Praise for Dawn

"Dawn is a gifted business / personal coach that has assisted in the development our staff, managers and myself in the improvement of our culture, team building and leadership. She has had a direct impact on our organization that has made a difference to our staff and bottom line. Dawn has the keen ability in her approach with people to establish rich meaningful relationships quickly. She uncovers all the possibilities and has a clear understanding to bring out full potentials. Dawn provides results for pro-active goal oriented success."

— **Michael Berger,** *Director of Human Resources at Mt. Elliott Cemetery Association*

"Dawn has helped my company achieve remarkable growth through her coaching. She has helped me make tremendous strides going from a short sighted business owner to a strategic thinking entrepreneur! Because of Dawn's leadership, my sales have continued to grow dramatically despite all the bad news you hear about the economy!"

— **Dave Cottrell,** *Owner of The Family Craftsman*

"As business owners, we all need accountability. Someone to help us formulate the next brilliant idea and someone to kick us in the butt when we are not paying attention to the bottom line. Dawn is that person. Systems run the business, people run the systems. Dawn will take you to the next level. All you need to do is follow her proven systems, have a passion to succeed and work hard. I guess if Tiger Woods can have a golf coach, I can have a Business Coach (and I have the best)."

— **Ray Cutway,** *Owner of Battery Warehouse Co*

"I clearly see the BIG VISION again, with one big difference; I now have a plan of action and am learning the skills to reach my goals. Hiring ClearVision has more than paid for itself. It has given us our best quarter in the history of our company with our revenues growing 469% over last year. I am excited to take this year head on, and experience explosive growth!"

— **Lynne Fiscelli,** *Co-Owner of Pane View Window Cleaning*

About Dawn Drozd

Dawn Drozd is the founder and CEO of ClearVision Business Coaching, a Michigan-based company specializing in helping business owners. A Certified Business Coach, Dawn has been named one of the Top 150 coaches in the world and Regional Breakthrough Coach of the Year, thanks to her coaching acumen and decades of experience as an owner of multiple businesses.

ClearVision works with business owners to increase focus, attract more business, develop their own dream team and significantly improve profits. ClearVision clients – across retail, service, financial, medical, and manufacturing sectors – achieve an average 40% + increase in profits and revenue.

For interviews or to book Dawn Drozd as a keynote speaker or workshop leader, please call (586) 323-5150 or email info@clearvision.us.com.

Find Dawn Online

www.ClearVision.US.com
Twitter: @clearvisionmi
Facebook: ClearVision Business Coaching
LinkedIn: www.linkedin.com/in/dawndrozd

The
Success
Code

9 Principles
for Small Business Success in Any Economy

Dawn Drozd

Published by ClearVision Media, LLC, Utica, Michigan.

This book is available at special quantity discounts to use as premiums and sales promotions, or for use in corporate or association training programs. To place a bulk order, please contact ClearVision Business Coaching at info@clearvision.us.com or (586) 323-5150.

ISBN 978-0-9914367-0-5

Printed in the United States of America.

Table of Contents

The
Success
Code

9 Principles

for Small Business Success in Any Economy

Dawn Drozd

Acknowledgements

I want to acknowledge and thank the many business owners who took time out of their very busy schedules to share their wisdom. Their combined years of hard work, trial and error, and sheer determination to keep moving forward during a time when many gave up, are what made this book possible. You are all heroes in my eyes and I wish you continued success for many years to come.

Introduction

As a country, we're big on business. And we're starting them at an amazing rate – more than 500,000 each year, or about one per minute.

These small businesses make a big impact, too. There are roughly 30 million small businesses in the United States, employing half of all workers in the U.S. and producing over $6 trillion in GDP each year.[1]

But, it's not all good news. If you're a small business owner, you're probably painfully aware that many start-ups fail. Across the U.S., small business failure rates rose by 40% between 2007 and 2010. That equates to more than 200,000 small businesses vanishing, taking with them in excess of three million jobs, according to census figures.

Bottom line – the economic downturn crushed the dreams of thousands upon thousands of entrepreneurs.

But there was good news, too. Not everyone failed. Some businesses, even those in industries that were hardest hit, continued to grow and prosper, and I wanted to know why.

So, in 2011, I started talking to successful owners whose businesses had continued to thrive, despite the downturn. I wanted to know how business owners operating in Michigan, one of the hardest-hit states, defied the odds during the worst economy since the Great Depression. What made their businesses stronger? How did they improve operations and grow revenue when tens of thousands went under? And, just as important, if those actions helped them survive during a down economy, what kind of impact would those practices have when the economy improved?

---

[1] Source: U.S. Small Business Administration, 2012

The only way to get answers was to go straight to the source. I spent 12 months interviewing over 50 small business owners who had steady or increased revenue between 2007 and 2011. They were all owners of companies in Metro Detroit with revenues ranging from about $1 million to $15 million with up to 250 employees (many were significantly smaller). As it was important to look at every industry, I covered retail shops, service providers, the building industry, manufacturing, and several others.

The results of my conversations with these gracious, helpful, and insightful business owners impacted me in a very profound way, because I truly didn't know what I would find. But after several interviews, I began to see a pattern that I knew was important – one that could change the focus of small business owners. It had the potential to impact their ability to more easily reach success. In fact, I began to see a very clear metaphor.

Imagine a vault. Inside the vault is everything that represents success to you: vacations, more time with family, donations to your favorite charity, retirement security, creating jobs – whatever it looks like for you. But the vault is locked and no matter how hard you try to get in, nothing works without the code.

Business owners throughout history have tried all kinds of codes to open their "vault of success." Some have cracked it, but most don't. Even when they keep their businesses open, many owners don't reach the kind of success they dreamed of during a good economy, let alone a downturn.

Interviewing these 50 business owners revealed the nine principles of the Success Code for small business. And now, the code is yours.

Because of this research, you will now know where to place your focus – on nine principles that, orchestrated together, can open your vault of success. I want to emphasize orchestrating them together. While each principle alone is incredibly valuable, the remarkable results happened only when the owners I interviewed executed all nine principles simultaneously.

Needless to say, I wish I had known these principles years ago when I owned my first business. It was 1991, and my husband, John, had a pastry arts degree. We both came from entrepreneurial families. John's dad owned a pizzeria in New York, and my father owned a funeral home in Michigan. And even today, my two sisters and their husbands own their own successful businesses. So when John suggested that we start a bakery, I thought it was a fantastic idea.

Now, at this point, we had three young sons – three-year-old twins and a six-month-old. And even though that was lots of work, we had big dreams and could envision our lives as successful business owners. Of course, that vision included making great money and having plenty of free time to spend enjoying life with our young family.

Sadly, we didn't achieve that vision. Despite John's baking expertise, two different location tries, countless hours away from our children, and years of hard work, we made the extremely difficult decision to close the business seven years after we started.

We were fortunate to sell the company for just enough money to get out of debt. However, the experience took an emotional toll on John. Over the course of those years, no matter how many strategies we tried, we couldn't get ahead. And I never understood why until I became a business coach in 2005.

It was then that I began to understand that it takes more than hard work and hope to keep a business going. It takes the right strategic focus, knowledge, and skills that I never dreamed we would need to run a small bakery. But, when you think about it, why should we have been surprised? Has information ever been exchanged so rapidly or the economy fluctuated so wildly? It reminds me of Dorothy's comment in The Wizard of Oz: "Toto, I don't think we're in Kansas any more."

But now, armed with the knowledge of the Success Code, I've had the opportunity to apply it to my own business and share it with my clients to gain better results than ever before.

There will always be dreamers among us who truly believe in our hearts that we can make our dreams of small business ownership come true. So why not ensure success? Why not learn from the best of the best, the people who, despite all odds, created profitable businesses in incredibly difficult times?

Let's be successful together and open your "vault of success." The code lies just ahead.

Unlock YOUR Success Code

As a business coach, one of my jobs is to help my clients take action. Unfortunately, I've watched hundreds of owners over the years learn new skills and have fabulous ideas, but never take action, leaving them stuck in neutral. Even if you read this book from cover to cover, it won't help at all unless you implement what you've learned.

So what gets in the way? Many things, but most common is not having a clear priority. Owners get so caught up in their day-to-day businesses that they never get around to identifying what's most important. But not any more. Now's your chance to make big things happen in your business.

To make it very simple, I've created a tool to help you get crystal clear on where you need to focus your time and energy. Constructed from the interviews with our most successful owners, my team and I built an assessment based on the nine Success Code principles. The assessment includes the exact practices our interviewees executed daily to create businesses that flourished even during one of the worst recessions in our history.

With the assessment, you'll identify your current strengths (those strategies you've already implemented and do well,) but more importantly, you'll also know what specific areas need attention in your business.

Armed with that information you'll be able to create a straightforward action plan that prioritizes your organization's resources and steps you toward implementing the most important Success Code principles.

To take the assessment, simply go to UnlocktheSuccessCode.com. When you're finished you'll receive your scores immediately and can unlock your own code to begin your journey toward more success than you ever imagined.

CHAPTER 1

Be an Intentional Leader

Being a business owner can be stressful during good times, let alone during economic downturns. Each year, 10% to 12% of firms with employees close. In 2009 and 2010, there were about 60,000 business bankruptcies.[1]

It's easy to focus on the urgent day-to-day operations and lose sight of where you're leading the company, or to become frustrated and stuck, not sure what direction to take. The owners in my research believed that in order to create long-term sustained success, they must have a clear vision for their company's future, their decisions must be well thought out, and their actions must be purposefully driven. Success requires both long-term strategic planning and shorter-term action planning, with unwavering, committed leadership and consistent communication to execute the plans that are created.

But take heart! Business planning doesn't have to be extensive and time-consuming. You simply have to regularly set aside time to reflect and answer these questions:

1. Where does your business stand now?
2. Where do you want it to go?
3. How will you achieve it?

What's Broken?

Before we can reveal how successful business owners achieved growth and profitability during the Great Recession, let's look at why so many businesses struggle with having an intentional plan. Here are the most

---

[1] http://www.sba.gov/sites/default/files/FAQ_Sept_2012.pdf

common reasons that I've found, from my own businesses and my work with clients:

- **The curse of the competent.** Many business owners excel at the technical or "production" side of what they do. They have remarkable skills in a particular trade or practice. This serves them well as employees in someone else's organization, but it can be a stumbling block in the path to growth and profitability in their own business.

  How can being technically competent hinder a business owner? Don't you need strong skills, especially in the lean start-up phase? Absolutely.

  But skills in delivering a service don't necessarily translate to skills in *running* a business. And many of us prefer to stay within our comfort zone, rather than exploring the messy and unproven areas.

- **Flying blind.** Many new business owners have no long-term vision – written down – to guide them (for personal as well as business goals). It's like boarding a plane with no guidance system. What's your destination? How will you know if you're getting closer or drifting farther away? Without a clear picture of your personal and business success, you'll never reach that destination.

- **Leaving your team in the dark.** If having a clear vision and a plan are the most important drivers of business success, then aligning and communicating goals with the entire company comes in a close second. Without goal alignment, even the best business strategy will flounder. Your team members won't know the endgame, so they aren't taking steps to align their actions with the big-picture goals. Employees who don't feel engaged in the company and its larger mission are less productive and are more likely to leave.

- **F.O.G. S. (fear of goal-setting).** Fear of goal-setting hampers many a talented business owner. It's not their fault. "How to set effective goals" isn't a class we take in high school or college – not even in business school itself!

  When you don't know how to set business goals, they're often poorly conceived. They may not align with an overall vision or may be too vague. And if you can't see a clear path – with milestones – to your goals, you won't ever reach them.

  Vague and unreachable goals are demoralizing for you *and* your staff.

- **Goals set adrift.** Then there are the business owners who set goals, but never look at them again. They don't know whether they came close to achieving a goal or failed miserably. There's no progress tracked, no learning from the attempt.

- **Short-term Steve/Sally.** This business owner only thinks or makes decisions in the moment, without pondering the long-term consequences or gains. That can have a disastrous effect. It's easy to live in the daily flurry of activity, putting out fires and never thinking about the long-term impact of your decisions or answering questions like these:

  - "How will giving this customer a discount impact our overall strategy?"

  - "What if we take on this project that our biggest client requested? What are the implications for the future? Will it help or hurt the business?"

- **No goal, no go.** Without a plan and goals, there's nothing to motivate the owner or the team. It's like living on a hamster wheel where each day is exactly the same – something to *endure* rather than *embrace*.

- **Faster burnout.** Running a business without regular planning heaps stress on the business owner, which leads to burnout. Lack of planning creates wasted efforts, poor results, and limited cash flow.

A 2009 Gallup Poll survey says that nearly half of self-employed Americans report working more than 44 hours in a typical work week, compared with 39% of American workers overall. "Self-employed Americans stand out as those most likely to work atypically long hours, in many cases upwards of 60 hours per week," says the survey.[2]

"Business owner burnout is one of the most common reasons for business owners to sell their business," says business broker Kevin A. Nery of The Nery Corporation. Even selling the business doesn't stem the bleeding. Nery points out that the effects of burnout impact the price you can expect when you're forced to sell.

"Unfortunately," he says, "many owners do not have their business ready to sell when burnout finally rears its ugly head. Business owners that do fall into this category usually will experience financial losses or a reduction in business value due to their inability to operate the business like they used to."[3]

---

[2] http://www.gallup.com/poll/122510/self-employed-workers-clock-hours-week.aspx

[3] http://www.gallup.com/poll/122510/self-employed-workers-clock-hours-week.aspx

Why It's Broken

Now, let's shift our focus from what's not working for small business owners to the reasons *why* those things aren't working.

Planning is a passion of mine. I knew the powerful impact it had on a business, but I was pleasantly surprised that my research revealed that it was a critical element for our interview subjects as well. I consider planning so important that, each quarter, I hold a business planning summit with my clients and invited guests. We spend an entire day reviewing long-term goals and objectives and creating 90-day action plans designed to achieve the goals.

Between these planning summits and my workshops, I speak with thousands of small business owners each year and, unfortunately, I hear lots of objections to planning. Let's look at the most common.

- **Goal novice.** Raise your hand if you took a class on goal-setting in high school. College?

  I didn't think so.

  As small business owners, we've never been taught how to set goals. It's something that we know we "should" do, but we just never get around to it because we're so busy doing things we are already good at (see "the curse of the competent" earlier in the chapter).

- **Tried that. Failed that. Done with that.** Some owners still bear mental scars from the effort of creating the original business plans they were told they needed, only to tuck them into a desk drawer, never to be seen again. Or the owner *did* set goals and created a plan that didn't turn out exactly like he hoped, so the whole process seemed pointless.

- **Seems cumbersome, complicated – and for "the big guys."** Amazon.com's virtual bookshelves are bursting with nearly 100,000 volumes on the topic of business planning. The mountains of information on the topic can intimidate any time-strapped business owner.

  When you're running an operation with a handful of employees, it can seem like overkill to set aside time and energy to work on planning for your business. You think, "Sure, GE, Wal-Mart, GM, and Apple practice business planning, but that doesn't apply to *my* situation."

- **Working in, not on the business.** A typical entrepreneur's trap is to continually be so busy working in the business that they don't have time for planning or working on the business.

- **No planning process.** Without an easy system to create a plan, most business owners default to constant activity mode, believing that they can out-hustle their competitors and the economy.

- **Flying by the seat of your pants.** Certain personality types run their own business because they love the high of "flying by the seat of their pants." Business planning forces focus and forward thinking that quashes the adrenaline rush.

  In the Kolbe Index, a test that measures a person's instinctive method of operation, business owners often score higher in the "Quick Start" action mode and lower in "Follow Through" and "Implementer" modes. Those who are bored by process dread staring at reports (or worse, *creating* them) and avoid the methodical work that goes along with implementing business plans.

- **Avoiding the truth.** And for a few, knowledge is uncomfortable and ignorance is bliss. If they haven't set goals, well then, they haven't failed to meet them either.

What Will Fix It

Chart your course for freedom and growth.

Whether the plans are sketched on the back of an invoice or created in planning software complete with color charts, our group of successful business owners (I think of them as Super Owners) all practice some form of regular planning.

They know where they aim to be in the next three to five years. They have goals and action plans to meet those goals. Following are some of their tactics.

Set an intentional future. Pick your destination and plan your route.

Let's say you want to drive from Michigan to Arizona. Without a map or GPS, you could end up in Washington, your time wasted and feeling less than thrilled to be there. The motive is simple: you plan for your business so you end up where you want to be.

But it doesn't have to be painful! There's no need for a 100-page binder or ten-step analysis. A simple process that you'll actually use is more valuable than any Harvard Business School-approved planning strategy.

Think you can't spare the time? You must, if you're serious about creating a sustainable business. Saying you're "too busy" can often be a self-fulfilling prophecy. Make sure you aren't making sacrifices you don't actually have to make. If your life or that of your loved ones depended on your willingness to carve out a few hours to create a simple plan for your business, you'd find a way, wouldn't you?

I'd like to share the simple planning process I use with my clients. It doesn't require any special training or tools – just time and a bit of thoughtfulness. And according to our research subjects, the payoff is completely worth the time investment!

This first step might surprise you. I tell entrepreneurs to start with *personal* long-term goals. This gets you in the proper mindset. Your business is a vehicle to get you the "life" you dreamed of; without reaching your own definition of personal success, having a "successful" business is just toil.

Long-term personal goals

While personal long-term goals are typically set three to five years out, it's helpful to consider what you want your life to look like at retirement age.

So, what's your long-term plan? Close your eyes and imagine retirement. Where will you live? How much income will you have? How will you spend your time?

Congratulations! You should now have some clarity around your lifelong goals.

Three-to-five-year personal goals

Now, let's move to those three-to-five-year personal goals. Your retirement dream may have been a little hazy, but these mid-term goals should be clearer. Consider having this conversation with your significant other, to make sure you share similar desires. Go ahead, pour a glass of wine and start imagining your future in just a few short years.

Start with six categories: Personal Finances, Experiences, Relationships, Community, Spirituality, and Health. (You can jump-start your goal formation by using the Dream Builder List I share with my clients. Go to the website, UnlocktheSuccessCode.com, and click on the big RESOURCES button. The Dream Builder List is a great tool to stretch your thinking and to help you to get clear on what you really want.)

Be very specific in each personal category. The clearer your goals, the more meaningful and believable they will be. For example, it's not enough to write that you "want to take a vacation." While that's a goal, it doesn't have firepower. Instead, paint a picture with details: you want to travel in an RV with your family to see the Grand Canyon next summer.

It's also very important to know the reason why you want to reach a goal. When writing down your goals, include your *why*, as well as how you'll *feel* when you've achieved the goal. The more powerfully you can tie the goal to an emotion, the more likely you'll achieve it. Here's that same goal, tied to a powerful emotion:

> *I want to travel in an RV with my family to see the Grand Canyon next summer. This goal is important to me because my parents took me there when I was a child, and I still have great memories of the trip. I want to build those memories with my children to bring us closer.*

Long-term business goals

Once you're clear on long-term personal goals across the six categories, it's time to determine your long-term business goals.

The owner of the most successful company in our study told me, "From day one of starting the company, I had the vision that there was a need to guide, train, and develop a specific group within the restaurant industry. I had a clear picture."

His clear vision, right from the beginning, has guided all his planning efforts.

For small businesses, "long-term" goals are typically based on a three-to-five year timeframe because things change too rapidly to plan further out.

Ground your long-term business goal setting by reviewing (or creating) your mission, vision, and values.

- **Mission:** The underlying purpose of your business – why it exists.

- **Vision:** How you want your business to look in the future.

- **Values:** Beliefs that you have about your business and the way that it should operate. These will drive your company's culture and be a framework for decision-making. Your business values will serve as a filter for hiring the right employees, too.

Write down these 10 business goal categories. You'll set goals in each of these categories:

1. Annual revenue
2. Profit
3. Number of employees
4. Number of locations
5. Breadth of services
6. Use of technology
7. Team quality
8. Industry reputation
9. Corporate citizenship
10. Debt position

Annual revenue, profit, number of employees and number of locations should be easily understood. For the remaining six categories, here's a bit of clarification:

- *Breadth of services* determines whether you will be offering different products or services to a different industry than you are currently serving. Is vertical integration your goal? Do you want to expand into related industries? For example, one of our study's business thrivers, the owner of an orthopedic practice, brought ancillary services in-house, adding revenue streams from ultrasound exams, braces, and supplements.

- *Use of technology* takes into consideration any technology that can help you do things faster or better, whether that's equipment in the office or in a technical aspect of the company. Another business owner, a commercial printer, makes decisions about new technology based on its fit with the mission and strategy of the business. His directive is simple: *"If it's a fit, you get it."* He says, "Without newer technology, we can't give our customers as many choices, and we aren't as efficient. The more efficient we are, the more we can do and the more competitive our pricing can be."

- *Team quality* covers technical skills and business skills, as well as aptitude/attitude. One of the most common practices among our business winners is a focus on team quality. Almost every company we interviewed made personnel changes to counteract the economic slowdown, ranging from layoffs in order to get lean, to hiring professional sales staff and motivating existing team members.

- *Industry reputation* asks you whether you want to be noticed in your industry as a leader. Do you want to stand out as a thought leader, speaker, or award winner? One of our orthopedics practice owners aims to control the geographic market as much as possible. His goal: "Be a big fish in a small pond."

- *Corporate citizenship* encompasses giving back through charitable cash donations, volunteer hours. and the like. The owner of a $2-million beauty salon and spa operation credits her business's community involvement for much of her success in surviving the recession.

- *Debt position* takes into account credit lines, credit cards, capital debt, etc. Not all debt is bad – sometimes it's necessary for expansion. Do you want to borrow to grow, or pay off any outstanding debts?

From goals to priorities

Once you've set some goals for your business across these 10 categories, it's time to think through the priorities that you'll need to focus on so you can reach the goals you set.

Make a list of about 10 priorities that align with your three-to-five year business goals. Don't spend a lot of time crafting them. They can be fairly vague, because you'll get more specific when you write your annual plans. For example, you might need to implement training programs, search for suitable space to expand, or develop new relationships within the community.

For example, our study participant who operates in a construction niche knew from his diligent research on trends that there would be an increased focus on environmentalism in the future, which would exert public pressure on his clients. In order to guide his clients, he certified in sustainable building practices and advised his clients on ways to improve their environmental practices.

Your long-term goals and priorities are now your guides in creating annual goals.

Annual planning

Just as with your three-to-five year goals, you'll create annual plans for yourself personally and for your business. Remember – the reason you're making business plans is to create the life you want!

Here's where you want to recruit reinforcements, too. Successful companies involve management and/or key employees to help determine goals, where possible. As the business owner, you may believe that your ideas are winners, but without the support of your team, goals can be doomed to fail. Let your team be a barometer for you; if the goals are too high or too low, they won't motivate.

Tom, the owner of the construction company, gathers his team leaders to help create the strategies to execute the visions he's developed. "By getting all their ideas and creative thinking on how we can make something happen," he says, "we create a stronger plan."

While you're crafting these annual goals, make sure they're *SMART*. You've likely heard this acronym. It creates a clear framework for successful goal-setting.

Goals should be:

- **Specific.** You need to know when the goal has been met. "Increasing gross revenue by 7% over the next 12 months" is specific. "Increasing sales" is not.

- **Measurable.** You'll want to track whether your actions are moving your business closer to achieving the goal.

- **Attainable.** Someone at some time must have achieved this goal.

- **Realistic.** The goal needs to be specific to you and the assets you control. Setting a goal to "add 200 new clients to your service business" may not be realistic if you're the only salesperson in your organization.

- **Timebound.** You'll need to know exactly when it needs to be done.

It's also important to determine the specific amount of growth you're setting as your goal because it will help determine the number and "strength" of the strategies you'll need to use to reach the number. A high revenue growth goal may require strategies aimed at gaining new customers and increasing sales to current customers.

After you've developed a list of goals, examine each one and ask yourself questions to cull the strongest, most effective goals:

"Is this goal aligned with the overall strategy?"

"Do I have the resources to achieve this goal?"

Once the goals are set, it's time to go back to your employees for their input. Ask them what focus the organization should have in reaching the goals. Creating that goal alignment – each employee knowing his or her role in achieving the goal throughout your organization – is one of the most important things you can do.

If everyone in the organization believes in the importance of the goals and sees a personal role in reaching them, much less "management" will have to happen. Here are a few benefits of aligning your team, goals, and strategy:

- Improves and accelerates business plan execution.

- Increases employee morale and improves retention.

- Creates ownership in the organization's success, resulting in more engaged (therefore more productive) employees. People are naturally wired to want to be part of something bigger than themselves. Harness that!

A study participant, the owner of a language learning company, commented that his leadership team believes that they are uniquely "meant to do this work." Now that's engagement!

Quarterly action plans

Quarterly action plans make the business planning process work. Too many companies stop after creating their annual plans, leaving that beautiful binder to languish on a shelf. The successful companies from my study and those that I've coached review their annual plans every 90 days and create quarterly action plans to help them reach annual goals.

This cycle works because it allows you to recalibrate every 90 days. It's systematic. You examine the progress you've made toward annual goals, evaluate projects and priorities that are working, and adjust or discard the projects that aren't working.

The language company uses quarterly action plans as the vital fourth component of its tiered planning system. The planning process kicks off with a board meeting to determine the high-level plan, then a leadership team meets to create goals "as if there were no limits," followed by the third step, a two-day facilitated leadership team planning session. In the fourth step, the leadership team meets quarterly to evaluate the success or failure of the previous quarter's plans, including the "who, what, when, why, and where" issues, and then creates plans for the next quarter.

Wondering what goes into your quarterly action plan?

You'll start with specific financial goals, such as revenue and profit numbers for each month. Then, outline the priorities and projects you'll execute to reach those goals. As an example, if you want to increase sales, you might plan a project to create a direct mail postcard campaign targeting a new market segment.

Once you've determined the projects (no more than 10, please!), it's time to add SMART goals to support those projects. If you were working on that direct mail postcard campaign project, for example, you might create a SMART goal to receive 50 phone calls from prospects who received the postcard. This gives your project a measurable business result.

Just like our annual goals and quarterly action plans, it's important for the team members who'll be involved to determine the projects. If the owner decides to do a direct mail campaign but doesn't get buy-in from his marketing director, it will be much more difficult to hold people accountable to the goal.

The final step in the quarterly action plan process is to break each project into smaller steps, with dates for milestones to be completed. This keeps the project on track. For our direct mail campaign, milestones with deadlines might include obtaining a target list, putting the call-to-action elements in place, writing the postcard content, designing the card, printing the card, sending the card, and executing your follow-up sequence.

While you're determining the steps of your project, include who is responsible for each task. This encourages teamwork and makes it easier to manage each project.

Be intentional

During the quarter, if a new project pops up, don't just add it to your list without thought. Execution requires smart planning, time management, and drive. Taking on too many projects can derail all of those. Make an intentional decision to replace a current project with the new one, or put it off until next quarter.

I advise my clients to keep a "parking lot" list for new ideas. This is a collection of ideas and projects that you evaluate each quarter. Having them in your parking lot stores them away without losing them and helps you avoid "shiny object syndrome" – getting distracted repeatedly with new projects and never completing them.

What if you *didn't* complete all the projects on your quarterly action plan or failed to achieve some of your goals? Relax. Examine those outcomes and *learn from them*.

Continue the growth cycle by reviewing your business's annual goals to create a new quarterly plan every 90 days.

What the code unlocks for business owners

My study of the nine principles of recession-proof business owners confirmed what I knew instinctively from my work with hundreds of businesses. *Sustainable, growth-oriented businesses are the result of careful planning, thoughtfully executed.*

Here are some road signs of effective planning:

- You have intentionally determined what your life and business will look like.

- You have buy-in from your family for your personal goals and from your employees for business goals.

- Everyone involved – family and employees – knows how they benefit from the goals and how they fit into the plans.

- Employees are mastering this new skill of planning. They are contributing to the planning process and even creating their own goals.

- Time management is more effective. Projects are being executed more efficiently.

- Fewer projects are falling through the cracks.

- Your reaction time is faster. You can more quickly evaluate a strategy or project and know if it's working.

- You have a record of achievement and can celebrate what you've accomplished rather than operating like a hamster on a wheel, expending energy without moving forward.

- You are reaching goals and learning from mistakes.

The first time you create your 90-day action plan, you may get excited and over-reach. So many owners are big thinkers. They don't include the details and don't estimate the real level of effort required. On the other hand, some owners are perfectionists who *under*-reach because missing deadlines scares them.

It takes practice! To estimate how many projects you can take on in 90 days, consider the effort needed and track the deadlines.

Review and celebrate

Schedule a review period at the end of each quarter. Outline everything that went right. Because you have your quarterly action plan with goals and milestones in writing, you can evaluate and appreciate all the things that went well. This isn't possible when you're "winging it." Give yourself and your team some kind of reward. Thank and congratulate other people for all that they've accomplished. Then, it's time to celebrate! Being a business owner is hard enough. Too often we're caught in the day-to-day pressure to do more. We need to stop and appreciate what we've accomplished.

My study documented what I knew to be true: successful business owners start with a clear vision for their business and make steady progress toward its achievement with intention and planning.

CHAPTER SUMMARY

Be an Intentional Leader

Key Points

Success Code Principle #1: Sustainable, growth-oriented businesses are the result of careful planning, thoughtfully executed.

- Your business will fail if you don't create plans for sustaining and growing it.

- There are many roadblocks you can avoid if you make clear plans, and just as many reasons why business owners stumble over these roadblocks.

- Before you set your business goals, you need to set personal goals.

- Business goals come in several flavors: long-term, short-term, and quarterly. Within each goal, you'll need to set priorities to keep you on track.

- Based on the size of your organization, try not to take on too many goals at once and be sure to make them SMART.

- You'll need to review your progress at the end of every time block so you can celebrate successes and learn from mistakes.

CHAPTER 2

Speak the Language of Business

We've heard the horror stories. Nearly half (49%, to be precise) of small businesses fail in the first five years, according to the U.S. Small Business Administration. Why? What goes wrong?

In his book *Small Business Management* (West Group, 1983), Michael Ames gives the reasons for small business failure:

1. Lack of experience
2. Insufficient capital (money)
3. Poor location
4. Poor inventory management
5. Overinvestment in fixed assets
6. Poor credit arrangements
7. Personal use of business funds
8. Unexpected growth

And Gustav Berle adds two more reasons in *The Do It Yourself Business Book* (Wiley, 1989):

9. Competition
10. Low sales

What do seven of these 10 reasons have in common? They involve tracking numbers!

For a segment of business owners, tracking and understanding the numbers in their business is a foreign concept. But it shouldn't be. Extremely rare are the stories of owners who achieve Forbes 400-level success without understanding at least basic financial principles. According to super-investor Warren Buffet, "You have to understand accounting and you have to understand the nuances of accounting. It's the language of business...."[1]

Even if accounting is a foreign language to you, tracking your numbers doesn't have to be onerous or time-consuming. (In fact, if it is, you may have a different problem.) There are a few key numbers that you must monitor closely to keep your bottom line healthy and your business sustainable.

Before we look at the metrics you must track, let's look at the reasons why so many business owners are flying blind at the helm of their own organizations without them.

What's Broken

As a business coach, I've seen both extremes: owners who either measure *nothing* in their business and those who measure *too much*. Either extreme can be limiting or downright damaging to the business.

Numbers intimidate certain business owners, so they measure nothing in their business. (Not surprisingly, this fear of numbers tends to afflict creative types more frequently than non-creatives.)

Then there's the opposite – those who measure too many things, too often. While creatives may avoid numbers, task-oriented types hunker down with paperwork to avoid their shadow activities: sales or employee relations. Too much measurement can suck all your time, and collecting too much data can actually obscure those few numbers that really "move the needle" in your business.

The worst offenders? The business owners who measure too much (because it makes them *feel* in control) but don't actually *use* the data to shape strategy or determine actions! It's a waste of everyone's resources.

---

[1] Warren Buffet and the Interpretation of Financial Statements, Mary Buffett, David Clark, Simon & Schuster, 2011, preface

Numbers drive decisions

The unfortunate consequence is that when business owners don't measure the right things, it becomes very difficult to make accurate, timely decisions. They're left to make decisions based on a gut feeling or an in-the-moment reaction rather than decisions supported by the numbers.

Hiring is an area where understanding your finances can have a major impact. When some business owners get busy, they hire staff. But it's not as straightforward as it seems. Perhaps a business owner should have hired earlier, and now her production is behind schedule and quality is suffering. The result? She's in a panic and willing to fill the role with any warm body. Or, let's say that as soon as she noticed more orders coming in, she added staff. But it was just a temporary blip, and now she can't support the additional overhead.

Numbers create the foundation for your business decisions

Many of the owners in my study were able to act quickly to correct for the economic impacts of the recession because they had a data trail, a history of numerical information they used to inform their actions.

"We were ready to buy a building, but we started to see our numbers softening up and pulled the plug on the purchase just days before we closed," said Steve, co-owner of a telecommunications firm. "I'm not sure what would have happened if we hadn't been paying close attention to the numbers."

The need to know your numbers applies to every type of business. A retail operation that doesn't accurately measure inventory may run out of items and lose sales. A sales team leader who doesn't measure the conversion rate for his salespeople will never know which members need more training or are in the wrong role.

Important decisions must be made every day if you're going to be successful, but it's hard to make them if you're operating in a cave without a flashlight. That's what not having accurate data is like.

The study participants didn't measure just to measure. They knew it was necessary to make smart decisions. "We don't wait to review our numbers after a week or a month. If we see three bad days of measurements, we're going to figure out what's going on and take specific action immediately," says Micky, a leader in a manufacturing company with tight margins.

Richard, the president of a $4 million specialty engineering and manufacturing concern saw the economic downturn coming before many other business owners. Reacting to the numbers in the business, he quickly reduced staff from 60 to just 25 people, shaved profits, and won every job the company pursued.

Other companies in the manufacturing space reacted more slowly, caught unaware by the creeping recession until it was too late. A 2012 report issued by the Information Technology & Innovation Foundation, a non-partisan think tank, says that 66,486 manufacturing establishments closed between 2000 and 2011.[2]

Cash flow woes

A huge number of businesses fail every year because they don't understand or have a clear picture of their cash flow. Cash is king in business, and if you aren't measuring your dollars on hand, you can't be sure of the financial health of the company.

It's simple. If you don't have enough money in your accounts from one

---

[2] http://www.itif.org/publications/worse-great-depression-what-experts-are-missing-about-american-manufacturing-decline

week to the next, your business can't survive. Inadequate capital is the number-two reason why small businesses fail.

How does this happen? Here's a scenario I've seen many times:

> The bootstrapping business owner doesn't pay herself much of a salary. She wants to invest all her cash in the business. After several months (or years) of scraping by, the business has a fantastic month collecting old debt. "Success at last," thinks the owner and pays herself a bonus.

> But within a few weeks, a big tax bill comes due and cash dries up. Since our business owner hasn't been tracking her cash flow numbers, she didn't anticipate the new expense. Now, she's strapped and can't meet payroll.

Why It's Broken

Let's start with a few general stats about small businesses. At any point in time:

> 40% of small businesses are profitable.
>
> 30% of small businesses are breaking even.
>
> 30% of small businesses are losing money.[3]

If you're not tracking numbers in your business, you won't know which bucket you're in (or which you're moving toward) until it's too late.

At the start of this chapter, I mentioned that business owners who don't measure anything in their operation typically have a fear of numbers. Recently, I worked with a professional photographer who loves shooting photos but absolutely hates the numbers part of her

---

[3] What's Behind High Small Biz Failure Rates? http://www.businessweek.com/small-biz/news/coladvice/ask/sa990930.htm

business. Tracking was akin to torture for her.

Some people measure numbers just because they think they're supposed to, but they never use the information. The numbers sit on a spreadsheet somewhere, never reviewed and sometimes never really understood. This is especially painful when a manager has tasked employees to gather data simply to gather data. It can be very frustrating and certainly isn't rewarding for the employee.

The same creative types who are uncomfortable with numbers also find measuring restrictive. They view financial and operational measurements as putting them in a box and believe that they can't change direction or plans once they've set a financial target.

Another number-avoider, the perfectionist, avoids vital financial tracking like revenue forecasting, fearing that if he tracks metrics like monthly sales or conversion rates, he'll be demoralized if his business fails to hit the target. Better not to measure at all.

Some don't measure numbers because they claim to be too busy doing other things. They don't see the value.

As with business planning, tracking numbers is another area that owners think is just for the "big guys." However, just the opposite is true. When cash flow is tight and decision-making is critical, one mistake could put your business under, so it's even more important for you than Fortune 1000 companies. Based on the research, the "small guys" *must* measure numbers or they're doomed to struggle needlessly.

The "ostrich" business owners let fear of disaster keep them from looking at the numbers in their business. It's as if not knowing makes the problem less real. But more often than not, the situation is not as dire as they think.

Diane, the owner of a medical equipment company shared this:

> *"You won't survive without tracking your numbers. We hired a chief financial officer and never would have made it without the numbers and error reports. We meet weekly to go over the numbers and strategize our next move. You have to know what you're dealing with."*

Accounting annoyances

Psychological barriers to tracking numbers aside, trying to keep track of your financial records, aka "accounting," can be confusing. Many items – like a Profit & Loss Statement and a Balance Sheet – can be called different names even though they're the same thing. When people are confused by something, they tend to ignore it.

Owners don't want to look stupid to their accountants, so they may not ask questions. Therefore, many don't understand the story their financial statements are telling them.

Some accountants (the kind I don't recommend) relish the control they have when the numbers confuse their clients, so they don't bother to explain them in layman's terms, holding the business owner captive.

Here's one of my personal pet peeves: when business owners use QuickBooks™ or a similar software program and *also* send the information to an accountant every month. The accountant makes a few minor changes to the numbers, creates a financial statement, sends it back to the business owner, and *charges* for the service. That's incredibly wasteful! I would much rather see the CPA tell the business owners how to set up QuickBooks properly, allowing them to generate the financial statements themselves.

The best CPAs and accountants see their role as consultants and advisors to business owners, giving advice on strategy and tax issues, *not* performing simple transactions. That's better done by a bookkeeping service at typically much lower fees.

The terminology of business accounting adds to the confusion, especially for inexperienced business owners. Whether you use an accountant or bookkeeper or a program like QuickBooks, you likely have a Chart of Accounts. This is a list of accounts used by a business to categorize the ways in which money is spent or received. It's used to segregate expenses, revenue, assets, and liabilities in order to give you, the owner, and other interested parties like banks a better understanding of the financial health of your business.

What's really confusing about having a Chart of Accounts is that there's no universal list of predefined accounts (at least not in the U.S.). Each accountant or business owner can create a unique list.

Then there's the question of allocating your expenses, revenues, and other transactions within your chart of accounts. How does the novice know which items go into what account?

Other troubles with tracking

Business owners may not measure certain areas within the business because it's really hard to do. For example, tracking leads in a business can be tricky simply because multiple people answer the phone.

Accuracy can be a challenge, too. For instance, if you're trying to measure how many phone leads you receive from a certain source, it's difficult to know whether your employee has remembered to log the information.

Personnel changes can undermine your tracking system, too. When there's turnover, non-critical activities can get lost in transition.

What Will Fix It

The bottom line is that too many owners don't know what to measure. Because there's no shortage of places to start, I want to give you a baseline and a framework so you can know what's important to measure in your own business.

The baseline

Start taking charge of your financial future by tracking the flow of money in your business. These basics are often referred to as "the financials" and include your income statement, cash flow statement, and balance sheet.

- **Income Statement:** Also known as the *profit and loss statement, P&L,* or *statement of operations,* this document lists your company's income (revenues or sales) minus your expenses, and it shows you the profit or loss over a specific period of time.

- **Cash Flow Statement:** A cash flow statement helps you know how much money came and went through the business for any period of time. Reviewing cash flow statements will help explain why you may not have the bank reserves you'd expect, even when your business is profitable.

- **Balance Sheet:** This is a cumulative document that lists your company's assets (cash in the bank, property, or equipment) and liabilities (loans you need to pay back) from the time you started your business. Reviewing your balance sheet gives you a snapshot of the financial strength and capabilities of your business.

Beyond the baseline: profit multiplier numbers

Once your financials are in order so you can produce them monthly, what else should you track in your business?

The answer can vary, depending on your type of business. But numbers that are measured in business are typically called Key Performance Indicators or KPIs. KPIs are used to assess the performance of your organization, a specific business unit, or an individual employee. To be useful in understanding and shaping business practices, KPIs must be measurable, understandable, and controllable.

There are literally hundreds of areas in a business that can be measured. In the Resources section of this book's website, UnlocktheSuccessCode.com, I've included a list of more than 100 KPIs, categorized by business function, such as sales and marketing, human resources, finance and business, health and safety, and environmental.

There also may be metrics from your specific industry that will help you improve performance. Often, industry associations can provide benchmarks for key performance indicators. One of our study participants, a telecommunications provider, belongs to an industry trade association where members contribute numbers to the association anonymously. The association then shares the pooled financial data to strengthen the industry as a whole. It makes sense to compare your company's numbers to those in the same industry rather than to companies in very different industries, because it's more likely to be accurate.

One example of this value is Revenue Per FTE (full-time equivalent employee). A company that specializes in cleaning marble and stone floors is labor-intensive – hundreds of employees, but only a few million in revenue. It's likely to have low revenue per FTE compared to an engineering firm with highly skilled employees and high margins, where the revenue per FTE would likely be much higher.

Since the same KPIs don't work for all businesses, here is a list of different businesses and the unique KPIs each one measured that correlate with the organization's success, as reported in *Inc.* magazine.[4]

Start-up computer consulting and contracting company:
Cash flow! "We have a bulletin board in the kitchen where we post graphs of cash flow and accounts receivable. We update it pretty much daily."

Production facility:
Ratio of shipments to budgeted sales. "If it's 100% or better, everybody knows it's going to be a good month."

Billable time as a percentage of total time; *billing points* (the points in a project when the customer can be invoiced).

Heavy-steel fabricator:
Gross margin per hour. "We're limited as to how many hours of work we can do in a month. So let's go after the projects that generate the most profit."

Inbound 800-line caller service company:
Call abandonment rate; calls per paid hour. "That second number makes us manage our people better."

Health spa:
"Ours is a sales-driven industry. We watch the *number of tours, the closing rate,* and *the daily sales.*"

Pallet manufacturing company:
Cost of materials. "We can affect that in a lot of ways such as how well we buy, how well we manage our scrap. It runs about 55% of selling price, so that's where the big bang comes."

---

[4] http://www.inc.com/articles/1999/12/15982.html

Food retailer:
Sales per labor hour. "We try to focus on the numbers that people can control."

Auto dealer:
"We're very strong on *customer satisfaction.* We think that's what ultimately drives the bottom line."

Photo processor:
Rework, which is a big factor in profitability. "Our rework numbers are posted and graphed weekly."

The most successful business owners in our study have a common practice – they tie their KPIs to the overall business goals and share them regularly with everyone on staff. They know that being open about the numbers fosters employee motivation and drive. When staff members understand how they can contribute to the organizational goals, they are more likely to do so.

Contrast that with certain leaders who use unfavorable financial results as a stick to spur employees to work harder – and maintain silence when the numbers are good. Secrecy breeds mistrust of management.

Sharing KPIs doesn't mean that you have to post every line of the company's Profit & Loss Statement or staff salaries, but your employees should know whether the organization is profitable, along with how well the company is performing in each of its critical areas.

KPIs: leading and lagging

There are two types of KPIs – *lagging indicators* and *leading indicators.* It's important to understand both and to use both in your business.

Lagging indicators measure the final result of activity during a specific timeframe. This could be sales produced by a postcard campaign. It's a lagging indicator because the activity is over and, even though it revealed whether the campaign was successful, you can't change the outcome.

Leading indicators, however, can predict the future outcome and serve as a "heads-up" for business impact. When you track leading indicators, you can predict an outcome more effectively. In the example above, the final sales from the postcard were our lagging indicator. However, the initial leads from the campaign were a leading indicator. If a large number of leads came in, our chances of driving more sales increased, making it important to take advantage of the leading indicator before it was too late to affect the outcome.

Let me share a simple example to illustrate this concept. Let's say that you wanted to lose weight. A *lagging indicator* is the number you see when you step on the scale. The weight is already determined. But measuring *leading indicators* – calories consumed and calories burned – is how you create the outcome you want: weight loss.

And here's another business-based example:

> Tracking product returns is a lagging indicator. However, tracking customer complaint trends over a specific period, such as a rolling 30-day period, allows you to fix problems before they impact the final result: increased returns. By noticing common issues across the complaints, you can clear them up *before* the lagging indicator of product returns is final.

Financial statements are both leading *and* lagging. They are lagging because when they're reported at the end of the month, the outcome can't be changed for that particular time frame. However, those statements are also leading indicators of your end-of-the-year outcome.

But what do I measure?

As we shared earlier, the range of metrics you should track in your business varies based on your business model, industry, and goals. However, there are two areas that are critical to measure within your organization: Financials and Sales Statistics. Why? Because without sales you can't build a company, and without profits your company can't continue to operate.

I'm hoping this discussion on the value of tracking numbers in your business has you convinced. But you may be wondering, "Where do I start?"

I've got a simple answer for you. If you aren't keeping updated and accurate financial records, start there. Each month, produce an Income Statement and Balance Sheet for your business. Also, if you invoice your customers and have to wait for your money, create a monthly Cash Flow Statement. Without accurate and timely cash flow numbers, the business can't survive.

When it comes to tracking numbers and creating financial statements, you don't have to use a software program like QuickBooks, but it can certainly make things much easier. Whatever software or tool you use, make sure you understand *how* to use it and that you are producing accurate information. I've known multi-million-dollar companies that ran spreadsheets parallel with their accounting software because the leaders didn't understand the software and couldn't get it to work "properly." That's a tremendous waste of both manpower and your financial investment in the software!

It's *critical* to fix a problem like that. Not only is it a drain on your resources, but you're exposing your business to unnecessary risk. Spreadsheets are too easy to manipulate, even accidentally, resulting in false data.

Which brings me to another cautionary note: who's double-checking your numbers? It's vital to have checks and balances. Even if you're relying on someone else within your organization to track the numbers for you, check them. Work with your accountant to make sure that the numbers are accurate.

What are your numbers telling you?

Once you have accurate financial data, you can advance to creating monthly financial statements and using them to identify challenges and opportunities within your business.

A challenge might be an expense category that suddenly increases. Perhaps your phone bill doubled last month. If you don't review your statements frequently, you could overlook a billing error. Or an expense could be recorded in the wrong category. Do the numbers seem unusually high or low? Compare the categories year over year to uncover potential mistakes.

Still another challenge is labor costs. Without close attention, labor costs can increase disproportionately and consume your profits. Periodically run a report of labor costs as a percentage of sales. If the number is creeping up, take action!

Perhaps a changing number reveals an opportunity. Your profitability is increasing, which means you can invest in that equipment that will expand your business by 30%.

Reviewing financial data can uncover opportunities in a service-based business, too. For example, in my company, we offer group coaching, individual coaching, and public speaking like workshops and keynote talks. By paying attention to which services bring the greatest revenue, I can focus on growing them further.

Budgets

Budgets are another very important financial tool. Many small business owners see budgeting as an exercise reserved for big businesses, but it's extremely useful for making decisions. The type of budget I recommend for my clients is a *cash flow forecast.*

This cash flow forecast includes the company's cash receipts and its disbursements – the money a company expects to take in and the amounts it expects to pay out as expenses. Basing your business decisions on a tool like this offers multiple benefits, because it:

- Predicts the effects before you actually add any kind of new expense or purchase (protecting cash flow).

- Determines how aggressive your marketing and sales activities need to be, based on your revenue goals.

- Offers a benchmark for future sales and expense goals.

The best way to create a cash flow forecast is to start with a spreadsheet. Include a column for each month. Show all the cash you expect to come into the business each month and all the cash you expect to go out of the business each month. (If you use QuickBooks or a similar program, export last year's numbers right into the spreadsheet.)

Now comes the fun part! Make a list of "what if" questions. What would our expenses be if we hired 10 more people? When can we afford to buy another vehicle? What would our profits be if we increased sales by 10%?

Fantasizing is fun, but the most valuable "what if" scenarios correlate to the annual plan you created in Chapter 1. Once you've listed your questions, enter the numbers that correspond to each question to make sure you like what you see in your forecast.

Not only will this exercise help you plan and make decisions more effectively, it can be incredibly motivating! When you see the financial impact that you can achieve with just a small change, you'll find strategies to make it happen. Plus, when you review your financial statements each month, they will have far more meaning.

Measuring sales numbers: the Profit Multiplier

Sales revenue in a company is typically a lagging indicator, like our weight on the scale. That means that if we want to predict what our sales revenues will be in the future, we have to identify exactly which activities drive the end results, the way that calorie intake and calories burned drive the number on the scale. The numbers that drive revenues will be your leading indicators.

In working with my coaching clients, I use a series of metrics that I call the Profit Multiplier Formula. The Profit Multiplier Formula was developed to identify those numbers that ultimately lead to revenue.

The six metrics I use with my business coaching clients are:
- Number of leads
- Sales conversion percentage
- Dollars sold per transaction
- Transactions per customer
- Customer retention
- Net profit margin percentage

Here's the exact formula:

Leads x conversion rate % = *number of new customers.*

Number of new customers + (existing database x retention rate) = *potential customer base.*

Potential customers x average dollar sale per transaction x number of average transactions per customer = *revenue.*

Revenue x net profit margin percentage = *net profit.*

(Download your own Profit Multiplier Worksheet at UnlocktheSuccessCode.com.)

While the formula is simple, having accurate measurements for each of those numbers is key to identifying opportunities for improvement. Once you know your numbers, you can determine how you'll improve them – whether it's with marketing strategies, training, sales process improvement, or something else. Without closely monitoring these KPIs, it will be much more difficult to predict upward or downward trends in sales.

What else should be measured?

I've talked about the importance of tracking your financials and monitoring profit multiplier metrics or KPIs. What else should you measure? The answer is, "It depends."

As I said earlier in this chapter, your business model, your industry, and your goals influence which stats you should track in your business. Here are a few guidelines to spur your thinking:

1. **Start by identifying problems or potential areas for growth in your operation.**

   Are sales lagging? Employee turnover too high? Would you like to reduce product returns? Improve profit margins on projects? At my website, UnlocktheSuccessCode.com, you can download a list of more than 140 metrics you could track in your business, organized under different categories: sales and marketing, employee development, recruitment, finance, health and safety, and environmental.

2. **Measure to create benchmarks.**
   Before you can improve an aspect of your business, you need to document its current condition. And often,

as soon as you begin to measure something regularly, you'll notice a remarkable side effect – the outcome will improve *without making any changes.*

This phenomenon is so well known that Karl Pearson, founder of the discipline of mathematical statistics, coined a maxim to describe it. Pearson's Law is this: "That which is measured improves. That which is measured and reported improves exponentially."

I see this happen frequently in manufacturing operations. During a client visit, I can look around the plant and see waste. Then, after the management team starts to measure waste, the amount is reduced, even though the processes haven't changed yet!

3. **Determine when to start measuring, how long to continue measuring, and exactly how to measure the performance you want to track.**
   This is critical. If possible, engage the staff members who will be directly responsible for improving the business area. Get their input on what should be measured and the best way to do it. Too often, we make it difficult to measure a process or event accurately, so the numbers we get don't paint a true picture of the situation.

4. **Determine how you will use the information.**
   Will the information be shared, kept private, or discussed with other staff members? If others are helping to collect information, get their buy-in by communicating how the information will be used.

Here are a few more things to think about once you begin measuring processes and activities:

- Determine the time period you'll need to measure. Certain activities, like a long sales cycle, may require tracking over months or years to benchmark and improve.

- Consider the impact of business cycles on your measurement. Are your sales seasonal? If what you're measuring will swing wildly, take that into consideration when reviewing the numbers.

- Determine how accurate the information needs to be and what that will mean for data collection.

- Once you start collecting the data, decide how often it should be reviewed.

There is no one-size-fits-all answer to the question of how often to review. As a general rule, leading indicators should be reviewed at least weekly because they are a predictor of longer-term results. However, when you're focusing on an area that's critical to the success of the organization, daily reviews may create the heat you need. Owners of a computer repair company that touts same-day service should know *daily* how the customers are being served, perhaps even by the hour.

Study participant Tom, who grew a business from his basement to more than $10 million in revenue in less than 10 years, sums up the basis for tracking numbers. He said, "The most important thing about execution is that you design a process that sets you up to make money. That's the goal. That's why you have a business. We've formulated our costs of goods sold, wages and overhead into a simple process that we use in every project bid without exception. It's worked out well for us every year we've been in business."

Knowing something about accounting and financial analysis isn't enough to make you Warren Buffet, but those skills can make running your small business more a pleasure than a struggle.

(Download my list of over 100 KPIs at UnlocktheSuccessCode.com.)

CHAPTER SUMMARY
Speak the Language of Business

Key Points

Success Code Principle #2: No matter how great your business is, you'll need to know your numbers.

- Numbers should drive all your business decisions.

- If you don't know your numbers, you won't know whether you're failing or growing.

- There are many reasons for ignoring numbers. All of them are bad.

- Even if your system isn't professional, your accountant will not think you are stupid.

- Learn how to create and maintain your financial statements.

- Determine all the areas where you can measure KPIs – there are more than you think!

- Learn what the numbers are telling you and act accordingly.

- Choose the stats that are critical to know for your particular business.

CHAPTER 3
Bring the Right Mindset

Being a business owner is not easy. I think of it like a Tough Mudder, an endurance event series created by the British Special Forces to test physical and mental strength. Participants run a 10-to-12-mile military-style obstacle course battling mud, fire, icy water, and 10,000 volts of electricity! A Mudder event is designed to test all-around strength, stamina, mental grit, and teamwork.

Just like owning your own business.

The official Tough Mudder website boasts that only 78% of participants successfully complete the event, but the outlook is far less rosy for businesses.

Today, only 71 companies from the original 1955 Fortune 500 list exist. Familiar, even beloved brands have been wiped out – Kodak, Circuit City, FAO Schwartz, and Michigan's own Borders are all tombstones in the business graveyard.

Entrepreneur Tanya Prive sums up the challenge in a Forbes.com article: "The nature of being an entrepreneur means that you fully embrace ambiguity and are comfortable with being challenged regularly. Choosing this career path is completely irrational because the odds of succeeding are dismal, but most succeed because of their unwavering belief, laser focus on delivering, and persistence."[1]

Prive knew what she was talking about. Our successful business owners also identified these three attributes as the key reasons why they remained successful when so many others failed. And they

---

[1] Forbes.com http://www.forbes.com/sites/tanyaprive/2013/05/02/top-32-quotes-every-entrepreneur-should-live-by/

proved over and over again that a mindset of unwavering belief, laser focus, and persistence is one of the keys to entrepreneurial success.

But it wasn't always so difficult to be a business owner. There was a time when you could learn a trade, hang your shingle, give decent service, and grow a successful concern that you could either sell or pass on to your children.

Not so now.

What's Broken

In today's fast-paced, incredibly competitive marketplace, you have to be on top of every aspect of your business: selling, marketing, hiring, firing, motivating, productivity, product development, finance, logistics, and more. The mental game of being a business owner has never been more challenging to play.

Let's survey what's changed in the small business world, in no particular order.

Competition. On steroids

As the population has grown, so has the sheer number of businesses in any community. Unless what you do is completely unique, you have more competitors than your business-owning forefathers ever imagined.

When I was growing up, my father owned a funeral home in Utica, a small suburban Detroit community. There was another funeral home in town, but we never thought of them as competitors. The reason was simple – one funeral home served the Protestant community, and the other the Catholic community. (Modern-day marketers would refer to this as "market segmentation.") There was no need to compete for customers. When it was your time, your religion dictated which funeral home performed your services.

Fast-forward 40 years and, boy, have things changed! Now, within the same geographic area, there are 10 funeral homes, none with a clear niche or unique position.

Information abounds

For centuries a business owner could count on dominating his local market, attracting the entire population that happened to reside within a certain radius and needed his services.

No more. Now consumers have access to goods and services from all over the world. The Internet and its abundance of information has made doing business more transparent. This means that some of the advantages businesses used to enjoy have disappeared in this new landscape.

Take buying a car. Pre-Internet, if you were interested in a buying a car, you'd schlep from dealership to dealership, looking at cars, taking test drives, and getting a sales pitch from each salesperson you encountered. The process could take weeks or even months. Your stress level soared as you tried to get the car and features you wanted at the best possible price…all without knowing what the "best possible price" actually was!

Compare that process to an approach recommended on Wisebread. com, a personal finance and frugal living advice blog:

> …you can email 20 dealers within a 50-mile radius, tell them what you're looking for, and ask them to send you back a quote. From those quotes, pick the lowest couple and take those to any dealership you want. They'll usually be forced to match it, destroying whatever profit margin they were hoping for. And

before you feel too bad, the dealerships get massive bonuses by hitting certain sales targets. They can give you the car at cost and still walk away with a nice pile of cash.[2]

Information advantage: consumer.

Global connectivity, global marketplace

People can now shop globally just as easily as they can locally. In fact, for many purchases, it's easier to buy from countries a world away with a click of the button. With the Internet and the Age of Amazon, that product manufactured in Bangalore is just as accessible as the one made in Bay City.

The global economy has positive and negative impacts on business owners. The burgeoning middle class in developing nations increases the demand for consumer goods. At the same time, growing populations mean a growing number of competing businesses, some with a distinct cost advantage.

It's standard practice to offshore manufacturing of certain products like electronic components. But now, even professional service functions like accounting can be performed by a skilled team tens of thousands of miles from you.

And oh, what changes social media hath wrought! Social media has given businesses a means to communicate directly with their customers, and that's leveled the playing field for smaller businesses against deep-pocket corporations. However, it's also given customers a platform to voice displeasure with brands and expect an immediate response to complaints. All in a public forum.

---

[2] http://www.wisebread.com/17-things-car-salesmen-dont-want-you-to-know

Now if you slip up, everyone knows. Make a snap judgment to flame your critics on an Internet review site, and the next day, you're the topic of all the morning news programs.

The speed of change

You've felt it. The pace of innovation and technology are causing monumental shifts in the way that goods and services are developed, purchased, and delivered.

In 2006, Facebook was a private network accessible only to college students, with 10 million users. Just six years later, Facebook has 1.1 *billion* users. Entire businesses are spawned or killed by Facebook.

A new technology that's attracting attention currently is 3D printing, a process that builds physical objects on a small printer by progressively depositing layers of melted plastic. Once the realm of sci-fi, this technology is on the verge of going mainstream. Prices for 3D printers are plummeting, with units available for $1,000 or less. Pundits and geeks alike are debating whether this technology really is a game-changer that will disrupt manufacturing and retail, but an article commenter points out that $1.7 billion in 3D parts were sold in 2011. The Boeing Dreamliner, the Mars Rover, and the Microsoft Surface tablet all have 3D-printed parts.

Brian Solis is a principal at Altimeter Group, a research firm focused on disruptive technology. A digital analyst, sociologist, and futurist, Solis has studied the effects of emerging technology on business, marketing, and culture.[3] He coined the term "digital Darwinism" to describe the effect technology can have on a business:

> We live in an era of "digital Darwinism," a time when technology
> and society are evolving faster than the ability of many

[3] http://www.briansolis.com/about/

organizations to adapt. It is this reason (along with a myriad of other problems, of course) that in fact killed Borders, Blockbuster, Polaroid, and the like. Not only did digital Darwinism cost us close to a half-billion jobs, it's only accelerating. As Leon C. Megginson once said in paraphrasing Charles Darwin's Origin of the Species, 'It is not the strongest of the species that survives, nor the most intelligent. It is the one that is most adaptable to change.'[4]

The most successful business owners in our research were the ones that were not only able to adapt, but were the quickest to do so. Why? Because they were positive and laser-focused every step of the way.

Business ownership has gotten more complicated

Way more complicated.

Now, if you want to remain competitive as a business owner, you have to be an expert in many different areas. It's not enough to be a good plumber. You also must know about employment law, tax law, marketing, sales, employee management, accounting, and coaching.

Before I began coaching businesses on growth, I was the marketing director for an apartment management company. We were just starting to use email for marketing. There were no smart phones, no Internet advertising (within the reach of small businesses), and no social media. It's impossible to imagine hiring a marketing director today who isn't proficient in mobile, Internet, email, and social media marketing.

The always-on culture has raised the service expectations of customers, too. Now, it's 24 hours a day, seven days a week for business owners. The businesses that aren't accessible lose out.

---

[4] linkedin.com/today/post/article/20130227142546-2293140-digital-darwinism-what-killed-borders-blockbuster-and-polaroid-and-how-not-to-end-up-like-them

Just a few weeks ago, Michigan's weather made its abrupt shift from winter straight to sweltering and I discovered that the air conditioning in my home wasn't working. Wanting to hire someone that I knew, I called a fellow Chamber of Commerce member. No answer. Not knowing when the business would respond, and wanting my air conditioning fixed, I called another company. These days, being responsive is often more important than price.

Constant pressure

Owning a business is a full contact sport. It can exploit every personal weakness you have.

> If you have relationship issues, it will affect your business.
>
> If you have confidence issues, it will affect your business.
>
> If you have health issues, it will affect your business.
>
> If you lack passion for your industry, it will affect your business.

Don't kid yourself and think that a successful business will miraculously fix your life and make you happy. (That's as delusional as people who think that getting married will improve their relationship problems.) In fact, all the new scientific research is actually proving that it's the other way around: a positive mindset – being happy – leads to success.

The opposite is true, too. Interestingly, being stressed or depressed actually affects a person's vision. When it grips you, you aren't able to see the possibilities for your own business. Creativity, brainstorming, and innovation suffer.

Sound like wishful thinking? Pollyanna-ish fluff that being happy will make you a more successful business owner and being stressed makes you less successful?

Nope, it's science.

Negativity hinders performance

Researchers in positive psychology, a new specialty focusing on the causes and effects of wellness, happiness, and success, have found that negative emotions actually narrow your mind and your thoughts.

Here's the evolutionary backstory:

> An oft-cited paper published by researcher Barbara Fredrickson (while she was with the University of Michigan's Department of Psychology) outlines the power of positivity on performance: "…positive emotions also produce optimal functioning, not just within the present, pleasant moment, but over the long term as well."[5]

> When our ancestors were faced with life-or-death situations, their heightened negative emotions acted as triggers to focus their thoughts on a narrow range of options: fight or flee. This involuntary reaction was useful when fighting off predatory beasts, but today it only diminishes our abilities. Now, when you're stressed about everything you have to get done today, you may find it hard to actually start anything because you're paralyzed by the length of your to-do list.

It's not my fault

Unfortunately, our culture has shifted from one of personal responsibility to one of blame and excuses. During the recession, it was far too easy to blame the economy for problems in our businesses, even if poor cash management practices or a lousy product predated the economic decline.

---

[5] The Broaden and Build Theory of Positive Emotions, The Royal Society, 2004

We fell prey to excuses during the recession. We convinced ourselves that we didn't have the power to overcome our business challenges. Even today, when things are improving, I hear excuses and blaming.

"If only we could find better people."

"If only I had more time."

"If only the government would back off."

While these all may be legitimate challenges, this victim mentality is truly dangerous. Like our Neanderthal grandparents, focusing on fear stops us from taking any action. It keeps us "playing small" because, deep down, we don't believe we have any control over our lives or our business.

Even large corporations can fall prey to blame-shifting and paralysis. Take Chrysler. The automotive giant ignored the signs of the upcoming recession, continuing to run what Forbes called its "bloated U.S. and Canadian operations."[6] The company limped along on government loans for several months until it was forced into bankruptcy in April 2009.

Contrast that with the companies in my study. Those business owners noticed the downturn coming and, like speedboats, nimbly adjusted course.

When Mitch, the owner of a collision repair shop, noticed the decline in revenues, he acted swiftly by downsizing staff, diversifying the type of vehicles his business serviced, and putting himself to work on the floor.

There were other small businesses that, like Chrysler, continued to

---

[6] http://www.forbes.com/2009/05/06/chrysler-gm-fiat-bankruptcy-opinions-colum-nists-nouriel-roubini.html

drift, ignoring the opportunities to pivot. In 2010, I met with the owners of an engineering company who revealed that their operation was in dire financial straits. They had no turnaround plans, telling me, "There's nothing we can do! It's just a bad economy. We just have to ride it out."

Where is that company today? Gone.

Trickle-down effect

Business owners who lack a positive mindset create a ripple effect in their own operations. Fear, anger, lack of confidence, and pessimism can create owners who:

- Can't make decisions.
- Bully their employees.
- Refuse to reprimand or coach poor behavior.
- Create a culture of doubt.
- Second-guess every decision made.

As a result, employees are disengaged, turnover is high, and little or no progress is made in any area of the business. Without the right mindset, it will be nearly impossible for an owner to grow the business past the start-up or what I call the "survival" phase.

Leadership expert John Maxwell, in *The 21 Irrefutable Laws of Leadership* (Thomas Nelson, 2007), talks about the "Law of the Lid." His premise is that there is a "lid" on a person's leadership ability, and the level – high or low - of this lid determines her level of effectiveness. This means that, for a leader, leadership ability determines the effectiveness of the entire organization.

I see the Law of the Lid as a metaphor. A new business is like a pot of water, but to get it to grow beyond mere survival, the water has to change and become something else; in our metaphor, it becomes steam. The owner represents the lid on the pot. The steam can escape only to the extent that the owner is willing to "lift" himself off the pot. The owner who has the wrong mindset will smother the expanding force, ultimately stopping the organization from growing.

How do you know when you're the low lid, stifling your organization's potential growth? You need a 360-degree evaluation of your leadership skills, performed with brutal honesty.

This isn't easy. It takes strength of character to acknowledge your challenges and work to overcome or compensate for them. That's why I admire my clients so much – they are willing to be vulnerable.

Why It's Broken

We've talked about the challenges that today's business owner faces and the importance of a strong, positive mindset in overcoming those challenges. Now, let's see how business owners develop the *wrong* mindset.

Not everyone is cut out to own a business

Business ownership may be romantic for some. We're a nation that reveres self-made men like Andrew Carnegie, Henry Ford, Richard Branson, and Bill Gates. We admire the too-rare self-made women as well. Just look at the media's intense interest in Oprah, Barbara Corcoran, and Sara Blakely.

To the "working stiffs," business owners seem to have autonomy, a constant source of cash, and the pleasure of bossing other people around.

The hype is everywhere – business consultants, trainers, inspirational CEOs, and glossy magazines like *Inc., Entrepreneur,* and *Forbes* collude to create a cult of entrepreneurship. "Start your own business. Be your own boss," they whisper seductively. "You'll have freedom. You get to keep everything you make!"

These publications and others like them skew the reality of business ownership. They typically feature business founders who've achieved phenomenal success – triple-digit growth, issuing public offerings, multimillion-dollar payouts.

To employees who never saw the hard work, mental toughness, and risk the owner endured long before realizing any measure of "success," those entrepreneurs may appear to have become rich quickly.

Another entrepreneurial myth perpetuated by the media is the role of venture capital investments in business growth. Not that it doesn't exist: VC is real. However, the impact and availability of venture capital on small business is greatly exaggerated. Stories of $10-million, $20-million, $50-million dollar investments in early stage start-ups distort reality. The truth is that only a fraction of a percent of all businesses receives venture capital funding. In 2010, venture capitalists invested approximately $22 billion into nearly 2,749 companies. That's less than 3,000 of nearly seven million businesses in the U.S.

Here's a more typical entrepreneurial success story: Tom, the specialty construction company owner I mentioned in the first chapter, started his company in his basement 12 years ago. Over the next decade, he grew the operation to $10 million through hard work, sacrifice, and four key components: vision, strategy, team, and execution.

The accidental entrepreneur

Sometimes we turn to business ownership because we can't find a job. It's a stopgap measure to avoid calling yourself "unemployed."

The recession killed 7.9 million jobs, the majority of those mid-wage occupations. A portion of those newly unemployed jumped into starting a business without really understanding what it takes, mentally, to own a business.

One of those was Patrick, an associate at a civil engineering firm. When cutbacks eliminated his position, Patrick saw it as an opportunity to scratch his entrepreneurial itch. He'd dreamed of the autonomy of running his own business, so he cashed in his firm shares and bought a silk-screening business.

Six months later, he was miserable. The margins on the silk-screened products were so low that he couldn't pay employees. Because he spent all his time working in the shop, he couldn't develop new business. And his plan to run the business with the help of his wife? She wanted no part of it. As soon as Patrick secured another engineering job, he sold the business at a substantial loss just to be rid of it.

That story is repeated thousands of times a month by smart people. Having been somewhat successful in their careers, they think, "How hard can it be?"

There's a misconception that entrepreneurs have a higher tolerance for risk than employed types. Not true. People who start businesses aren't necessarily more optimistic than others; often, they just don't see the risks inherent in starting a business.

Lack of confidence kills

I like to say that people use a formula: Be x Do = Have. We possess some idea of what we want to have or accomplish, and we go about staying busy or doing what we think needs to be done to get those things. However, we miss who we have to *be* as people to sustain our well-being and help reach our goals.

The *be* part of the formula represents the identity and beliefs we hold true; who we truly believe we are. Henry Ford said, "Whether you think you can, or you think you can't – you're right." If deep inside we have doubts, insecurities, or a paralyzing fear of making mistakes, business ownership will be extremely difficult.

A person who's toiled for wages in someone else's company may fantasize about running his own company. When he's laid off years later and opens his own business, his self-image as an employee, not the boss, follows him.

It's like multimillion-dollar lottery winners who suffer from "sudden wealth syndrome."[7] Despite their new riches, they hold a self-image of a person who struggles financially. Now, throw in the fact that many lottery players have below-average incomes and limited financial literacy. They don't think of themselves as wealthy people or people who are savvy with money, so they never learn to manage their wealth.

Who, me?

Putting the blame on circumstances is easier than taking ownership of our shortcomings. Most of us were raised to believe that making mistakes is a bad thing, something to be avoided if possible. In elementary school, I remember raising my hand eagerly to answer a question, only to get it wrong and have the entire class laugh at me. That lesson is repeated over and over again during our young lives.

The lesson carries over to our adult world, too. For example, business failure is viewed particularly harshly in the Midwest. While Silicon Valley looks at failure as valuable experience, it's a stigma in Middle America. The message seems to be "fail once – give up forever."

---

[7] http:// www.investopedia.com/terms/s/suddenwealthsyndrome.asp

Not everyone gets a trophy

We have a different problem when our parents tell us we're good at everything we do, and we're rewarded with trophies for participation rather than performance. Both practices teach us that making mistakes is bad. Rather than being encouraged to learn from them and continuously improve, we're either reprimanded or rewarded for mediocrity. So, as adults, what have we become? A society that makes excuses, blames others, or is in denial when things don't go according to plan.

How "more and faster" creates the opposite effect

What else hinders entrepreneurs' mindsets? The "B" word: burnout. In our culture, we fetishize working long hours and forgoing vacations. Self-denial and exertion are strains of our Puritan legacy. According to an article on CNNMoney.com, "U.S. workers received an average of 12 vacation days in 2012, down from 14 in 2011.... And, of those vacation days, they only took 10 of them off."[8]

More numbers: according to a Wells Fargo/Gallup poll, "Today's small business owner works an average of 52 hours per week, with 57% working at least six days a week, and more than 20% working all seven. Small business owners surveyed take an average of two weeks of vacation per year, with 14% not taking any vacation at all. Of those taking a vacation, 39% do work-related activities (phone calls, emails, etc.) during that time."[9]

An owner I know was so frazzled that after only three years, he was ready to close for good. He was working 70 hours a week, pouring his own money into the company every month to make up for cash shortfalls, having difficulty keeping employees, and struggling to cope with the toll it was taking on his marriage. Burnout had struck with a vengeance.

---

[8] http:// money.cnn.com/2012/11/16/pf/americans-vacation-time/index.html

If you burn out in a corporate environment, you can fix the problem by switching jobs. A disappointment, sure, but there's significantly less at stake than for a business owner who has heart, soul, and resources tied up in a company.

If you burn out in a business venture, it's typically the result of intense pressure building up over time. It's infinitely harder to walk away, because that would mean abandoning your dream, leaving your employees jobless, and possibly facing dire financial and psychological consequences.

What Will Fix It

With the catalogue of trials testing the mindset of entrepreneurs, how did the Super Owners of our study outperform their peers so dramatically? There's no one prescription that guarantees business success. However, during my coaching with hundreds of business owners and my study of the 50-plus CEOs who survived the recession, I've uncovered a few key mindset traits the most successful shared.

They stay focused on the positive.

These thriving entrepreneurs all have their own version of this mantra: "I believe we can grow." For them, it isn't blind wishful thinking. They all have a deeply held belief in their company and their ability to weather the economic storm.

Their positive mindset might be what leads them to creative plans for sales and growth. Remember the research I mentioned earlier in this chapter that linked negative attitudes to a narrowed focus, which limits creativity?

---

[9] More than Half of Small Business Owners Work at Least Six-Day Weeks, Still Find Time for Personal Life, Wells Fargo News Release, August 9, 2005, https://www.wellsfargo.com/press/20050809_GallupPersonalLife.

It turns out that the long-term effects of *positive* emotions have an even bigger impact on success. Dr. Frederickson conducted experiments to prove that positive emotions broaden your sense of possibilities and open your mind, which in turn allow you to build new skills and resources that can provide value in other areas of your life. Ahem, like business.

Harvard University-educated professor Shawn Achor, who now teaches for the Advanced Management Program at the Wharton Business School, talks about the "happiness advantage":

> *… your brain at positive performs significantly better than it does at negative, neutral, or stressed. Your intelligence rises, your creativity rises, your energy levels rise.*
>
> *In fact, what we've found is that every single business outcome improves. Your brain at positive is 31% more productive than your brain at negative, neutral, or stressed. If we can find a way of becoming positive in the present, then our brains work even more successfully as we're able to work harder, faster, and more intelligently.[10]*

They believe in their organization/purpose.

Jason, the founder of a company that develops language learning software, says that he and his employees share the belief that they were "meant to do this." As a team, they follow their passion and align it with products they believe can be the best in the world. That passion drives them to give great service, innovate, and power through any challenges.

They take ownership for everything they do.

Blame has no place in business. Sometimes that means stepping up

---

[10] http://www.ted.com/talks/shawn_achor_the_happy_secret_to_better_work.html

and getting your own hands dirty instead of urging your employees to work harder. When Mitch, the owner of the collision repair business, cut employee overtime to reduce expenses during the worst of the recession, he also put himself to work in the shop. Sharing the burden inspires your team to devote their best efforts, too.

Mike, the owner of a heating and cooling company, has a similar attitude: "As the owner, it's my job to go get the business."

During the recession, they were honest and let their employees know they were concerned, but never insinuated they wouldn't make it. More than half of the high-performing companies I studied reduced staff or hours during the recession. While none said it was an easy decision, they all believed it was the only way to save jobs and ensure the company's long-term survival.

The leadership team sets the tone for the entire organization, especially when communicating unpleasant information. "Our attitude was, there is no way we're going to go out of business," said Steve, the owner of a $4-million communication company.

They listen to employees. And they nip gossip and negativity in the bud.

Knowing that gossip creates discontent among teams and kills productivity, our successful CEOs moved swiftly to stem it. They understood that in the absence of information, people will fill the void with their own perceptions and opinions.

Personal finance guru Dave Ramsey has a no-gossip policy in his organization. His mantra is, "Negatives go up, positives go down." Anyone who has a complaint or issue should only send it up the chain, never down. Complaining to someone who can't solve the problem is not tolerated.[11]

They take time out to have fun with their teams.

Instead of cutting training and team-building activities like most companies during the recession, Jason kept them going. "Our leadership team has had a lot of positive feedback about taking the team off-site for the day and doing simple team-building exercises."

Another leader occasionally takes his entire staff on boat trips as a reward for hard work.

They regularly communicate with their teams – through formal and informal means.

Our leaders know that employee engagement is one of the main drivers of company performance. Employees who are engaged in the company and in their work are more productive and stay with the organization longer.

Steve, the owner of a telecommunications company, leads the sales team on a conference call each morning for 10 to 15 minutes for a quick check-in and accountability. It's the same with the operations team, where project managers meet once a week. These calls and in-person meetings are critical for keeping the information flowing up and down in the organization.

Ryan, the owner of a contracting company, buys lunch for his in-house staff once a week to discuss new ideas and ways to improve.

They take time off – completely unplugged – to rejuvenate and relax.

Too many of us, especially business owners, are juggling and feeling overwhelmed. Paradoxically, the best way to get more done is to spend

---

[11] http://www.cumanagement.org/article/view/id/NextGen-Know_How-Combat-ing-Negativity-and-Gossip

more time doing less. Our study participants knew this.

A February 2013 *New York Times* article reported on the benefits of unplugging:

> A new and growing body of multidisciplinary research shows that strategic renewal – including daytime workouts, short afternoon naps, longer sleep hours, more time away from the office, and longer, more frequent vacations – boosts productivity, job performance and, of course, health…[12]

Stanford researcher Cheri D. Mah found that when she convinced male basketball players to sleep 10 hours a night, their performances in practice dramatically improved. Free-throw and three-point shooting each increased by an average of 9%.

More vacations are similarly beneficial. In 2006, the accounting firm Ernst & Young did an internal study of its employees and found that for each additional 10 hours of vacation that employees took, their year-end performance ratings from supervisors improved by 8%. Frequent vacationers were also significantly less likely to leave the firm.

They surround themselves with positive people.

When these business owners feel stress or creeping pessimism, they talk to people who will lift them up – whether it's business or personal connections.

The people we choose to associate with have a powerful influence on our own outlook and success. In fact, Jim Rohn, one of the early leaders of the personal development movement (big names like Tony

---

[12] http://www. nytimes.com/2013/02/10/opinion/sunday/relax-youll-be-more-pro-ductive.html?_r=0

Robbins and *Chicken Soup* mogul Jack Canfield credit Rohn for their own success) said, "You are the average of the five people you spend the most time with."

For business owners, the five people often include employees. You wake up each day and spend 8+ hours with your team. They can become as close as your family. It's important that they support your positive attitude, not sink it.

They use motivational tools (DVDs, live seminars, CDs, books) to remain positive.

Nearly all the Super Owners in my study told me that they regularly seek out opportunities to boost their own outlook and motivation.

I personally have a monthly subscription to *Success* magazine. Each issue comes with a CD containing interviews with people who have achieved a measure of success in their field. I listen to these in my car while driving to meetings and speaking engagements. The continuous flow of positive messages gives me fuel for my own work.

They are honest with themselves about their own shortcomings and take action to improve them.

It's simple. When you take action, you feel much more in control and positive. Psychologists call this having an "internal locus of control." The locus of control is determined by the extent to which you believe you have power over events in your life. People with an internal locus of control believe that they can influence events and their outcomes, while those with an external locus of control blame outside forces for their circumstances.[13]

Author, scholar, and organizational consultant Warren Bennis

---

[13] http://psychcentral.com/encyclopedia/2009/locus-of-control/

is widely regarded as a pioneer of leadership studies. When he interviewed great leaders to find out the characteristics that made them superior for his book, *On Becoming a Leader* (Basic Books, 2009), the interviewees all agreed on one idea: leaders are made, not born, and made more by themselves than by any external means.

Operating a business tests an individual's mettle. Those who made it through the recession are true leaders; they were successful because of their unwavering belief, positive outlook, and persistence in the face of challenge.

CHAPTER SUMMARY
Bring the Right Mindset

Key Points

Success Code principle #3: A positive attitude and unwavering belief in what you do is critical. It's needed to keep everyone moving forward in pursuit of your goals.

- Science has proven: positive mindset = positive profits.

- Believe in yourself and your business.

- Take ownership for everything happening in your life.

- Stay connected with people who have a positive mindset.

- Take time out to have fun and enjoy life.

- A successful business won't fix your life, but a positive attitude will make everything better.

- Avoid blame-shifting. Never become a victim.

- Remember: Be x Do = Have.

- Be honest with your employees, but stay confident in the outcome.

CHAPTER 4
Get Efficient and Stay that Way

Here's what we know for sure: the world is moving at a faster and faster pace, and the successful owners in our study ensure that their companies remain efficient and fully productive so they can stay ahead of the competition.

That means using the technology they have to its fullest capacity and upgrading that technology when it makes financial and operational sense.

But technology is only one side of the productivity equation. Employees are increasingly required to do more with less, so our successful owners find ways to encourage their teams to be more efficient to remain competitive and profitable.

While you have been reading this book, there have been hundreds of changes in the technology world. You might have heard of Moore's Law, a maxim describing a driving force of technological and social change in the last 50 years or so. In 1965, Intel Corporation co-founder Gordon Moore observed that, over the history of computing hardware, the number of transistors on integrated circuits *doubles* approximately *every two years*.

The upshot? The exponential improvement in computing power has dramatically expanded the impact of digital electronics in nearly every segment of the world economy.

From Ma Bell to iPhones

Did you think you'd see the demise of the newspaper or get rid of your "home phone"?

When I was growing up, my household and all those in my

neighborhood had *one* telephone. The service was delivered through hard wires, strung to telephone poles on your street. It was also corded, tethering the user to the location where the phone was installed. Fast-forward to 2008. Even then, not only did most individuals in a household have their own phone, but 20% of American households had only a cell phone – no landline! That percentage climbed to 35.8% in 2012, according to the National Health Interview Survey. (And in the under-30 crowd, *60% of households* are cell-only.)[1]

Copper-wire voice lines and television sets are disappearing. And with them, entire businesses are disappearing or reinventing themselves.

Not only is the technology changing, it's transforming how we live, work, and play.

Amazon's Kindle is an amazing device that allows avid readers to carry hundreds of books around in their pockets. Even the most ardent dead-tree book lovers have been lured to digital through sheer convenience. But the Kindle revolution is about more than the fact that I'm reading pixels instead of ink dots on printed pages. Beyond its tremendous storage capacity, Amazon's ecosystem has changed the way that I *acquire* books.

The old method: when I was bored or got a hankering for a new read, I'd visit a bookstore, roam the stacks, flip through pages, and select a few for purchase. This happened a couple of times each quarter.

The new method: someone mentions a great book she just read. Within 60 seconds, I've logged into my Amazon account, searched the book title, and pressed the "one click" button to purchase and

---

[1] http://gigaom2.files.wordpress.com/2012/12/wireless201212.pdf

download it to my Kindle. That's 60 seconds from discovery to digesting the book's contents.

To avoid being displaced by this book-buying phenomenon, brick-and-mortar bookstores have to offer something different to consumers…an experience that websites can't replicate.

The same is true in your business. Either you go the route of Amazon and integrate technology that gives your operation a price, delivery, and service advantage, or you create a spectacular experience for your customers. And if you want to be like Bonnie, owner of a travel agency and one of our outstanding CEOs, you combine technology growth with service levels that exceed your customers' expectations.

Here's the bottom line: because information is changing so fast and competition continues to grow, you can't afford to ignore new technology. It's necessary to stay competitive.

History is rich with examples of businesses that ignored new technology – at their own peril. The Eastman Kodak Company is best known for making photographic film products. From its start in 1888 through most of the 20th century, Kodak dominated the photography market and, in the mid-1970s, had a *90% market share* of photographic film sales in the United States. Yet, in 2012, Kodak filed for Chapter 11 bankruptcy protection.

How did Kodak go from almost a century of market leadership to bankruptcy in 30 years? It's simple: Kodak ignored new technology. Their struggles began in the 1990s when consumers' preferences shifted to the convenience of digital photography.

Even if you know that your business needs to use technology to remain competitive, that's not enough if you buy without a technology implementation plan, if you don't get the necessary training, or if you fail to fully use your new equipment's capabilities. And even if you get all those things right, you can still fail on the people side by not engaging your team in productivity.

What's Broken

Some owners buy the latest gadgets, software, applications, etc., without really knowing how to use them. They mistakenly believe that this new technology will be the panacea for their business ills.

However, if there's no plan to integrate the new technology and use it to significantly improve operations, it becomes the latest "flavor of the month," gobbling up resources instead of providing a real solution to a problem.

Prestige ≠ productivity

Business owners can fall victim to the lure of technology as a status symbol, too. Like flying first class, buying the latest software program or suite of iPads for your staff gives you the *illusion* of business progress, but these alone won't make your team more productive or drive higher dollar sales.

Hard habits to break

Changing habits is extremely hard work. Changing your business operations is infinitely harder. Which is what makes learning and integrating new technology one of the ultimate business challenges, but it's one that you must master.

Technology used "a little" is technology wasted

Some owners never use the technology they already have to improve their efficiency. Tools languish on desks and in server rooms, becoming obsolete.

Here's a common software implementation story: one of my former clients purchased a sophisticated software program designed as an all-in-one customer relationship management (CRM) system, order processor, and inventory management tool. The company believed that it would improve operations, but they never created a plan to integrate it into business practices. After the initial installation, they went through a brief training, but then didn't use the system for months because they "didn't have the time" to disrupt their operations and work through the learning curve.

The project I was helping them with ended and unfortunately when I checked back in, the staff was still using approximately 10% of the system's capabilities. Instead of using the expensive system to its capacity and wringing out the financial investment, the management team continues to create dozens of spreadsheets that can't share data between their desktops and the new software system. The result? Where the company could be saving efforts, they are duplicating them.

Even when there's a pretty clear case that the technology – say, adopting a sales management tool like SalesForce.com – is a long-term productivity enhancer, its own beneficiaries (the sales team) may oppose it rather than change their behavior.

Multibillion-dollar corporations and the federal government are not immune to the pitfalls of wasting money on unused technology either. According to an article on TechRepublic.com, back in 2008, the country's biggest trash hauler, Waste Management, filed a *$100 million lawsuit* against an SAP, a large maker of enterprise software for managing business operations and customer relations, for "failed implementation of SAP's ERP (enterprise resource planning) package."

And from ComputerWorld.com, November 2012: "The U.S. Air Force has decided to scrap a major ERP software project *after spending $1 billion*, concluding that finishing it would cost too much money for too little gain….the project has racked up $1.03 billion in costs since 2005, 'and has not yielded any significant military capability,' an Air Force spokesman said in a statement."[2]

A consultant who analyzes ERP failures said, "…software often fails to achieve its promise due to the reluctance to change by people who have a vested interest in existing processes."[3]

However, even with properly implemented technology, productivity may still stagnate because all the technology in the world can't fix bad management.

People side of productivity

The fight for survival during the 2007–2009 recession prompted many companies to scrutinize the people side of the productivity. With little excess revenue to spend on complex technological advancements, business owners looked to increase productivity through their human capital. It makes sense, right? A small increase in employee productivity can create big contributions to the bottom line.

Before we talk about how our thriving business leaders leverage their staff to improve productivity, let's look at some reasons why companies fail to get the value from their employees.

Breaking up is hard to do

When a staff member isn't performing, "nice" owners sometimes feel it's easier to hold onto a person than to let them go. The owner hopes that a little motivation or the right training can transform a lackluster staffer into a strong contributor. That rarely works and, most often, it's a failure with far-reaching ramifications.

---

[2] http://www. .computerworld.com/s/article/9233651/Air_Force_scraps_massive_ERP_project_after_racking_up_1B_in_costs

[3] http://www. reliableplant.com/Read/10733/real-reasons-why-erp-systems-fail

So why aren't these people fired? Here are three reasons:

- **Sympathy.** In a small business, employees and employers know each other well. It's like a family. Heck, often we know each other's families, too. And who wants to fire a family member?

  By letting the employee know the issues and giving him a chance to correct them, you avoid surprises. My advice is to approach the situation with a mindset of service; if you wish to serve your employees well, you won't keep them in jobs where they can't be successful. Use compassion to help these people transition out of your company.

- **Overwhelm.** Dreading the time and effort required to hire and train a replacement employee causes some owners and managers to keep poor performers too long. But a stellar performer will get up to speed quickly and will then outshine the mediocre performer for years.

- **Morale concerns.** Worry about the negative reaction of other employees to a firing keeps some lackluster performers on the payroll longer than warranted. Instead, owners should worry about how *keeping* a poor performer impacts morale. Employees want their leaders to expect, notice, and reward results. Tolerating poor performers undermines the idea that the organization holds high standards for its employees. There are huge opportunity costs to not having stars in every role.

Productivity can be hard to measure

Manufacturers have it easy in one respect. Managers can measure the productivity of individual workers by simply dividing the number of hours a person works by the number of widgets they produce.

But in knowledge-based organizations, it's not so simple. After a piece of software has been created, how should a manager measure the value that each participant contributed to the process?

The challenge to measuring productivity in a knowledge-based business is linked to knowing what and how to change to become more productive and therefore more profitable. Managers and business owners must identify the actions and behaviors that lead to the greatest revenue so they can be replicated in other employees.

Billable hour backfires

Most professional service businesses, such as law firms and engineering companies use billable hours to measure productivity. Each hour that an employee is able to charge to a client is tracked. Employees compete and are rewarded for billing as many hours as possible each week, each year. This gives a sort of measuring stick, but relying solely on billable hours can create its own problems.

Basing pay and bonuses on billable hours is a disincentive to improve efficiency (why would someone want to finish more work in fewer hours?). It encourages bill "padding" and workaholism – where quality suffers. The cult of the billable hour also traps these firms into commodity-based pricing – clients making buying decisions based on the firm's number of hours-per-project – rather than value-based pricing.

The web changes the rules

When it comes to business efficiency, few technological advancements can match the impact of the Internet. Global connectivity has flattened the competitive markets, making it unnecessary to buy locally. And while some business owners are marketing their products and services to the global economy, there are still many owners who don't know how to do that or are afraid to try.

A business owner I know sells electronics accessories in a retail store. For years, her small website functioned as a digital brochure, containing general information about the items she carried, store hours, and contact information – but no e-commerce capabilities. A customer who wanted an item had to visit the store to make the purchase. In the last few years, her healthy revenue eroded because competitors entered her market and are now actively selling through their websites.

Social media burst onto the scene in the early 2000s, becoming a dominant marketing tool. Suddenly a start-up business with five full-time employees had the same ability to grab a potential customer's attention as a billion-dollar conglomerate.

David vs. Goliath, with razor blades

Gillette, a division of Procter & Gamble, is a +100-year-old company that has completely dominated the men's razor market. It continued to release new product after new product, each more expensive than the last. In 1999, the company was reportedly worth $43 billion. It seemed untouchable.

In 2012, along came the upstart Dollar Shave Club. According to an article on FastCompany.com:

> Armed with little more than an engaging YouTube video, a direct-to-consumer approach, and a message that stands in stark contrast to competitors' selling propositions (nearly give the razor away at the expense of a high-priced blade addiction), the company is positioning itself as an up-and-comer in the $13-billion men's shaving industry. It enlisted 12,000 customers in just the first two days its e-doors were open.[4]

---

[4] http://fastcompany.com/1835082/3-marketing-takeaways-dollar-shave-club's-fing-great-ad

A wee little company (Dollar Shave Club started with five employees) with a great business model, fueled by a YouTube video that's racked up nearly 11 million views is putting market share scare into the $43 billion behemoth. Talk about efficient productivity!

All hail the power of social media, indeed.

The big boomer shift

A shift that gets less public attention than social media but may have just as big an impact on business is the "big baby boomer business shift." Right now, more than 50% of small business owners are between 45 and 65, and many of them are preparing to sell their businesses. In fact, according to WealthManagement.com, there are 12 million boomer business owners, and 70% of them will retire over the next two decades.[5]

A survey by Pepperdine University and two trade groups, the International Business Brokers Association and M&A Source, showed an uptick in business sales at the end of 2012 and early 2013.

"It was almost like a light switch went on in January," says Michael Schuster, a broker with World Business Brokers in Miami. "We started getting a lot of activity with sellers who said, 'I don't want to go through another downturn or tough time. I want to see if I can sell my business.'"[6]

The trend of baby boomers selling their businesses will continue. Once the pent-up demand for purchases has been absorbed, the balance will shift to a buyer's market with 8.4 million businesses changing hands! Understandably, many owners who are looking to get out don't want

---

[5] wealthmanagement.com/retirement-planning/here-come-boomer-biz-owners

[6] http://smallbusiness.yahoo.com/advisor/retiring-boomers-drivng-sales-small-businesses-185659061.html

to take on the added risk of new purchases or big changes before they sell. But is this undermining the value of the business, ultimately diminishing the price it could command?

"You have owners who are ready to retire, but the business is worth half of what it once was, so they've been holding off on selling. Now that the economy is starting to get better, the value of the business may be rebounding, but they will all want to get out at the same time," says Bill Entwistle, a Rhode Island-based financial planner who advises many small business owners.[7]

Are you thinking about getting out in the next 20 years? Take heed: if you haven't differentiated yourself from your competition, put smart processes in place, and honed efficiency, you may not get the price you want.

Why It's Broken

Productivity, technology, and superstars on staff – if the formula for profits and growth is so simple, why do the majority of small businesses struggle and fail? Let's look at some of the challenges.

No money, no tech

Not only did the recession depress business valuations and keep retirement-ready owners at the helm, it stalled investments in technology. Struggling owners stopped buying new equipment and pushed technology updates off as long as possible to conserve cash. That's left some operations woefully out of date.

Lack of planning

I believe in the power of planning. A well-thought out plan, well executed, can increase a company's profits by 50% or more. But too

---

[7] wealthmanagement.com/retirement-planning/here-come-boomer-biz-owners

many business owners are flying by the seat of their pants. Racing to put out fires, they don't invest the time to plan for the next quarter, the next year, the next three years. As a result, the owner doesn't know what technology or equipment will be needed in the future. With no plan, tech investments are made on the fly and without the proper forethought to integrate them into operations.

Overwhelmed with speed of change

I started this chapter with stories of businesses being buffeted by change. That rate of change is increasing exponentially. New companies start. Business "institutions" die. Products and services that were revolutionary a few years ago become obsolete unless they adapted to market changes quickly.

It's no wonder that many small business owners are reluctant to make major investments in new technology tools or in changing systems. Few owners feel confident in their ability to predict what lies ahead on the business horizon.

Technophobia

Half of all small businesses owners are over 45 years old. For every tech-savvy boomer, there's a handful of compatriots who find themselves befuddled by technology.

Others avoid adding new technology, not because of their age but because of their mindset. They're stuck in the "this is how I've always done it and I don't want to change" trap.

Nowhere to turn

Having a mentor or coach has helped some business owners push past the tech investment stumbling block. But business owners without a trusted advisor have few options for information and insight. Competitors aren't eager to spill the secrets to their competitive advantages. Family members don't have the perspective to offer constructive ideas. Where do today's business owners find answers?

Perfection paralysis

Certain personality types are afraid to make decisions. They're looking for the "perfect" solution, so they stay stuck with old technology and outdated operations. This dynamic creates the "paralysis by analysis" syndrome.

At an engineering firm in southeast Michigan, the senior leaders have been "working on" an incentive system for employees for over eight years. The incentive program, which is designed to encourage and reward staff members for bringing new business, isn't in place because it's not foolproof *yet*.

And it never will be.

Systems? What systems?

I've talked about some of the most common reasons that small business owners don't invest in technology or fail to wring the advantages from it. Even more fundamental, there are businesses rife with waste because they lack systems. Without standard practices and systems, time is wasted and business operations suffer. Employees can't contribute at the highest level.

Some clients are in this situation when we first start working together. The owners are skilled at a trade or service and have grown their business through sheer hustle and iron determination. But now *the business is running them*. It's become the tyrant boss they once dreamed of escaping.

Often, the first areas we tackle in the business are the internal operations. Here are some of the problems I frequently see:

- Nothing is written down. Business activities are performed without standards. And employees are constantly reinventing the wheel.

- There's no accountability or follow through. If nothing is written down and there are no systems in place – well, those tasks you asked a staffer to complete three weeks ago probably aren't done. And you won't know until it causes a breakdown.

- Accountability isn't just measuring tasks, however. It's measuring results. Too many business owners get it wrong. *In Managing the Future* (Plume, 1995), business guru Peter Drucker said, "It's not how quickly we can check off the items on an action punchlist or how thoroughly we can respond to an audit or how well we fix errors found by the quality assurance department. It's how few punchlists, audits, or defects there are to deal with."

- Drive-by delegation. Giving an employee an important assignment as you're jogging past them in the hall is not real leadership and won't ease the pressure on you. What will? Clear instructions, accountability, and follow up.

Death by meeting

If you want to tackle one of the easiest ways to improve your business operations, start with meetings. In my work with small businesses, I've found that meetings typically are either non-existent or poorly run.

A Microsoft Office Personal Productivity Challenge survey of 38,000 people in 200 countries found that people in the U.S. spend 5.5 hours each week in meetings, and 71% of respondents feel that meetings aren't productive. That's more than 12% of work time consumed by a non-productive activity (respondents worked an average of 45 hours per week.) What would happen in your business with a 12% *increase* in productivity?

The age of distraction and the myth of multitasking

With so many communication options – both traditional and tech-enabled – we have so many more ways to be distracted. Our discipline hasn't yet caught up with the capabilities, so instead of using it to be more productive, we're wasting more time than ever.

Checking email, texting, and surfing the web during meetings gives us the illusion of multitasking, of being productive. The truth is that our brains are not wired to function this way. Our brains process concepts sequentially.

Brain Rules (Pear Press, 2009) author John Medina says, "To put it bluntly, research shows that we can't multitask. We are biologically incapable of processing attention-rich inputs simultaneously."[9]

How much less effective is your brain when you attempt to multitask? Worse than if you had just smoked a joint! A 2002 Carleton University study found that marijuana dropped smokers' IQ by 4 points. Researchers at the Institute of Psychiatry at the University of London studied 1,100 workers at a British company and found that multitasking with electronic media caused a *greater decrease* in IQ than smoking pot or losing a night's sleep – a drop of 10 points.[10]

While it's scary to think that multitasking makes you dumber while you're doing it, what about the impact it's having on your decision-making ability?

---

[9] http://forbes.com/sites/carolkinseygoman/2011/04/26/the-myth-of-multitasking/

Constantly responding to electronic interruptions is to fall victim to the tyranny of the immediate, not the important. Business owners who are multitasking are never prioritizing the essential work that needs to be done. Which means that it seldom gets done.

Lack of training

Another obstacle to peak efficiency is that small businesses often don't have training processes. People work in roles with no job descriptions. New employees are expected to train themselves, absorbing how to work efficiently through osmosis.

Going solo

Want to know what the highest-performing athletes at every level have in common? They all have coaches. Serena Williams, Wayne Gretzky, Derek Jeter, Lindsey Vonn, Tiger Woods, Tom Brady – players at the top of their game still rely on coaches to help them continuously hone their skills and improve execution.

So why do so many business owners opt to go it alone when it can be so dangerous? According to *Small Business Management* (West Group, 1983) author Michael Ames, lack of experience (a flaw that could be remedied with coaching, which lets you benefit from *someone else's* experience) is the number-one reason why small businesses fail – not to mention the productivity improvements that inherently take place when a coach is holding you accountable.

What Will Fix It

Now let's turn to what entrepreneurs are doing *right* to get efficient and stay that way.

---

[10] http://articles.chicagotribune.com/2010-08-10/opinion/ct-oped-0811-multi-task-20100810_1_iqs-study-information-overload

Learn how to learn

The superstar business owners in my study were continuous learners. They were constantly looking for changing dynamics and trends that would impact their industry.

Jim owns an $11-million plastics manufacturing operation. He wears his role as chief learner as a badge of honor, "We have tremendous knowledge of our product and our industry."

Attention to daily details keeps his company profits steady. "We measure manufacturing numbers in the plant like waste, productivity and efficiency," he says. "We track costs daily and measure sales and quotes monthly."

Ryan, president of a $5-million contracting company, says he and his staff are always developing and looking at systems. "We track every job by the hour, and our project managers have daily numbers they need to hit."

Jason, president of the language learning software company, knows that technology developments will have a big impact on his customers. As consumers shift to mobile devices, his company has developed apps for iPhones, iPads, and Android devices.

To get more, get out

Breakthrough business ideas aren't sparked by continuously sitting behind your computer. To burst into being, they require the friction of other people. To really absorb your clients' struggles and collect new ideas to improve business operations, you need to mix it up. Participate in trade shows and conferences; find associations that will keep you abreast of technology changes.

Tom, the basement-to-$10-million Super Owner, estimated that he devotes 25% of his time to reading, researching, and being active in his clients' associations. He sees his company as the industry leader, which means that he needs to be able to predict the trends that will have an impact and to guide his clients through the changes.

Try new things, quickly

Instead of being mired in outdated processes, successful companies have a culture that recognizes positive risk. You can't be afraid to make mistakes – you *will* make them.

In *Business Brilliant: Surprising Lessons from the Greatest Self-Made Business Icons* (HarperBusiness, 2013), author Lewis Schiff shares unconventional beliefs of self-made multimillionaires, based on 12 years of research. The belief that's important for this chapter is #7: "Setbacks and failures have taught me what I'm good at."

Here's how Schiff explains it:

> *Those who are "business brilliant" have, on average, more failures than members of the middle-class. But they use those failures to help them succeed on the next attempt. Just 17% of the middle class say they learn from their failures in this way, which is really a shame. Everything worth trying contains an element of risk, after all. If you fall on your face, you might as well learn from the experience to help you succeed on your next try.*[11]

The important thing is to *fail fast*. Management guru Tom Peters said, "Test fast, fail fast, adjust fast."

Rather than waste months or even years analyzing and debating whether to buy a new piece of technology, restructure your

---

[11] http://www. inc.com/lewis-schiff/habits-strategies-of-ultra-wealthy.html

organization, or try an incentive system, test the new idea, evaluate it, and adjust it.

Thriving CEO Richard, who heads a specialist manufacturing and engineering firm, has long been an early adapter of the latest technology. He shares the attitude, "Let's take this risk and figure out really quickly if it's going to work."

Jim, the plastics manufacturer, is constantly seeking ideas to give his business a competitive advantage. He says, "We look at new technologies on the Internet, and we talk to suppliers. We're not afraid to try new things."

Stay open-minded

Having an open mind as a business owner means letting go of control. That can be scary for some, but it brings its own rewards. You'll be able to continuously seek and discover new ideas, new opportunities, and new solutions to the challenges you face.

Hire techies

You don't have to keep up with all the latest tech trends personally. Expand your company's capabilities by hiring people who are comfortable with emerging technologies. You'll complement each other's strengths.

Invest in human capital

Speaking of your team, remember that providing training for employees *increases* retention. Instead of treating training and development as an expense, look at it as an *investment* that will increase your team's efficiency and creativity.

Have a culture that recognizes positive risk

Every business has a culture, a system of values and behaviors throughout the organization. Does your business culture recognize and allow for risk? If your culture is risk-averse – where new ideas are shot down and unsuccessful attempts are punished – you're handicapping your company's success.

Take your cue from a little company called Google. Co-founder Larry Page had this to say when an employee made a major mistake: "I want to run a company where we are moving too quickly and doing too much, not being too cautious and doing too little. If we don't have any of these mistakes, we're just not taking enough risk."[12]

If that's a little radical in your world, listen to what Joe, a great CEO and owner of a tooling company had to say: "Sometimes you have to take a risk. You have to take a look at all the components and say, 'This is the best thing to do.' So be cautious, but then be passionate when you pull the trigger."

Have a plan to invest in it

Savvy business owners make sure their annual business plans include investing in technology to boost productivity and growth. Those investments involve time and training, as well as dollars.

Look for what others can teach you

While some entrepreneurs run their companies with a lone-wolf mentality, the thrivers believe in learning from other companies, even from those in the same industry.

Case in point: the owners of a small window-cleaning company attended a conference where they met owners of several larger similar businesses. Over the next year, the small business owners stayed in touch and gained valuable insight into the processes technology use of

---

[12] http://www. fastcodesign.com/1672718/6-ways-to-create-a-culture-of-innovation

the bigger companies. When the small company expanded its services from residential to include commercial window cleaning, they got advice on the equipment and systems they'd need. Learning curve shortened!

Verbon, a plumbing and heating wholesaler, could have viewed big-box home improvement stores as his company's enemy. But instead, he joined forces with them: "We decided if you can't beat 'em, join 'em. So we partnered with a local big-box store because we had expertise they didn't have. They are happy to refer those customers to us."

Steal from other industries

There's a common misconception that businesses need a unique idea to be successful. The fact is, most businesses are not based on an innovative idea – they're based on a mundane idea executed well.

Even some of the greatest "innovators" in history were actually more like "improvers." Henry Ford didn't invent the automobile. Thomas Edison didn't invent the electric light bulb. Those things had already been invented, but weren't accessible to the masses. Ford and Edison changed that. Both were highly talented *improvers*.

Rather than seeking the illusory innovative idea, look to proven concepts in other industries. Take your cue from Ford, who in his quest to create "a motor car for the great multitude," borrowed ideas from meat-packing and grain mills.

A PBS program reported:

> *He and his team looked at other industries and found four principles that would further their goal: interchangeable parts, continuous flow, division of labor, and reducing wasted effort...*
> *In 1913, they came together in the first moving assembly line ever used for large-scale manufacturing. Ford produced cars at a*

record-breaking rate. That meant he could lower the price and still make a good profit by selling more cars…[13]

Paul, owner of a payroll company, learns a lot by going outside of his own industry. "We've even reached out to higher education to remain cutting-edge in data management."

Systems help you and your team follow through

It's easy to get caught up in the "shiny object syndrome." There are new ideas, new technologies, and new initiatives, any of which could take your company to the next level. But if you constantly try new things without following through, you'll never see big results.

The formula for executing on your ideas and keeping your business continuously improving? It's what Chapter 1 of this book was all about – creating a plan and then working that plan. My clients who do this consistently reap steady growth and increased profits.

To motivate your team, focus on results, not tasks

Daniel Pink, a researcher and author of the *New York Times* bestseller, *Drive: the Surprising Truth about What Motivates Us* (Riverhead Books, 2011), says that autonomy is a key driver for people. He points to a Cornell University study of 320 small businesses showing that those that offered autonomy grew at four times the rate of control-oriented firms and had one-third the turnover.[14]

Bottom line: when you tell your team the result you expect but allow them to determine the means and mode of achieving it, your team will be happier, more motivated, and more productive. Who doesn't want that?

---

[13] http://www.pbs.org/wgbh/aso/databank/entries/dt13as.html
[14] http://www. marshallcf.com/assets/book_reviews/Drive.pdf

Ask your team for ideas

This goes hand-in-hand with our previous point. If you want continuous improvement, you need to ask team members on the front lines for their input. Do they have a better way to approach the problem? A tweak to the system?

Ask, and then listen.

Get on board or get out of the way

It might feel mercenary, but you *must* get rid of dead weight in your organization. If an employee is unwilling to embrace change or discuss new ideas, help them exit the organization.

"Aggressive on technology" is how Bill, one of the owners of a business-to-business communications technology company, describes his policy. But they don't ignore the people side of the equation. "During the recession," he says, "we upgraded people, hired different expertise, got more training. It allowed us to go much deeper with our clients, product, and service."

Do the research

Before you invest in new technology, figure out how the new tool will integrate into what you're already doing. What other technology is affected? Will you need to change any procedures?

Just don't get mired in research! Printing company owner Peter cautions, "You can research forever, but unless you're an expert, you'll have to trust other people to give you good advice." If your organization is large enough, assign a team member the job of staying on top of industry and technology trends, like Jason did in his language learning software company.

Be aware of how technology is shaping your industry, but also the individual business components of your organization: customer service, marketing, sales, operations, finance, etc. Are vendors using Electronic Funds Transfer (EFT)? Are more of your website visitors expecting robust web chat capabilities for customer service?

Listen to your customers

Customer demand is the driver for Peter, who says, "If we can't do what the customer wants, we have to figure out how to get it done. If new technology fits the mission and strategy of the business, you get it."

Get the proper training

Investing upfront time in training (hint: more than you think you need) will pay dividends later. You'll need two types of training – technology-specific training and systems or process training. Don't skimp on either one.

Remember my story at the beginning of this chapter about the company that is using only 10% of its all-in-one customer management, order processing, and fulfillment tool? Those owners are stepping over dollars to pick up pennies. The smart investment is to devote time and dollars to improve long-term efficiency and productivity in your business!

Find a shortcut? Take it!

As a business owner, you can't be married to your process. You have to be agile, always looking for a faster, cheaper, easier way. Watch out for perfectionists and process-oriented personalities who can stay stuck doing something the same way over and over. Because they're comfortable using a spreadsheet to store contacts, they refuse to use the CRM that would save time.

Even little ideas can yield results

Improving efficiency in your business is more incremental than revolutionary. You don't have to hire an efficiency expert to improve productivity.

Sherman, the owner of the waste management company, believes in continuous improvement: "Our systems are easy to follow, up-to-date, and always improving. It makes a huge difference."

Let's say that you're not sure a process is working. Here's a low-tech but extremely effective exercise that will help you re-engineer it.

1. Choose a process in your business and grab a stack of sticky notes.

2. Write each step of the process on a sticky note, one step per note.

3. On the wall or on the floor, stick the notes in the order that you follow to complete the process.

4. Now, gather everyone who is impacted by the process and ask them to study the steps. Can you move a step? Or more than one? Does it make sense to combine steps? To skip steps? Reorder steps, eliminate some, or combine some, and determine how those changes will affect your process.

This method makes it easy to visualize and change steps, as you explore the ramifications of your reengineering ideas. It's much more dynamic than making a computerized list of steps, and it taps into our heightened ability to absorb information visually.

While increased competition, changing technology and managing employees for improved efficiency challenge today's small business owner, our study participants found ways to meet those challenges, with profitable results.

CHAPTER SUMMARY
Get Efficient and Stay that Way

Key Points

Success Code Principle #4: To stay ahead of the competition, be sure your company is efficient and fully productive.

- Because information is changing so fast and competition continues to grow, you can't afford to deny that new technology exists and is necessary to stay competitive.

- Get the most efficient technology that you can afford and learn how to use it.

- Even with the best technology, you can still fail if you don't engage your team in productivity.

- Find the best way to measure productivity with your new systems.

- Many out-of-date businesses run by boomers may be on the market soon.

- If you need a technology coach, hire one!

- Even when we're aided by technology, multi-tasking wastes time.

- Invest in your employees' training (and your own).

- Encourage sensible risk-taking. If you fail, fail quickly and then adjust.

- Be ready to retool a process that's served you for some time. There's always room for improvement!

CHAPTER 5

Embrace Sales

Owners who are successful in tough economic times execute specific sales strategies. They spend more time rekindling relationships with previous customers, invest in salespeople with proven track records, research and capture new markets, measure all activity, and continuously invest in sales training. They recognize that blaming the economy for decreased revenues is a luxury they can't afford, and they make every effort to continuously move forward, even by small amounts.

When owners don't understand sales and don't engage themselves in the sales process, it's usually disastrous. The business world has become far too competitive, and the buyers are much more sophisticated. Sitting back and waiting for business to come to you just won't work.

As the recession started, many owners were faced with a shocking new reality: sales had stopped flowing. These entrepreneurs struggled because they'd never had to "sell" before. For some, by the time that they got involved, it was too little, too late. Their lack of sales strategy, planning, and execution was the final nail that sealed the coffin on their business.

Success can kill resourcefulness

Those rare entrepreneurs who stumbled into profitable and abundant revenue streams early in their business ventures were at a disadvantage when the economy tanked. Lulled by years of success, the owners never developed tracking mechanisms to know *how* or even *where* the sales were coming from. They didn't try new strategies and evaluate the results because they'd never had to do so. They just assumed that the sales would continue pouring in, no matter what.

Around 2008, I met with a company that – like so many based in metropolitan Detroit – supplied automotive parts to the Big Three. The recession had struck, and the owners were paralyzed. As makers of precision cutting tools, they were capable of diversifying into non-automotive fields, such as medical. But they didn't.

"Yes, we know we *could* diversify, but we aren't sure how to go about it. We just don't know if it will work," the owners told me. Their action plan? "We're just going to ride this out and keep doing what we do well."

Having started the business when the automotive industry was thriving, these business owners were spoiled by success. Fundamentally, they weren't making sales – they were taking orders. And when the orders stopped flowing, so did the revenue.

Ultimately, the company (barely) survived by filing Chapter 11 bankruptcy, reorganizing, and eliminating most of the staff. But other companies waited too long to save themselves. According to analysis by the Business Journals of U.S. Census Bureau data, the recession killed more than 170,000 small businesses from 2008 to 2010.[1]

Contrast that scenario with another manufacturing business, whose majority shareholder I interviewed for my study. Just like the Chapter 11 filers, this business was entrenched in the automotive sector. However, *before* the economic circumstances became dire, Joe and his partners took action to diversify the client base from solely automotive to include manufacturing parts for the aerospace and defense industries as well. As a result, they stayed strong.

---

[1] http://www.bizjournals.com/bizjournals/on-numbers/scott-thomas/2012/07/reces-sion-claimed-170000-small.html

Early success can make business owners complacent. Michael Ames, author of *Small Business Management,* whom I've mentioned in previous chapters, lists "lack of experience" as the top reason that small businesses fail. However, I want to modify that business-killer with a deeper insight of my own: It's not just *experience* that's necessary for business success – even owners with experience can fail. Experience alone doesn't make you better equipped to run your business, just like living in a cave doesn't make you a geologist. Only *evaluated experience* can make you better.

What's Broken

Many owners start their companies because they're good at the technical aspect of their industry. They're talented lawyers, plumbers, doctors, engineers – but they don't like to "sell."

They think:

> *"I'm an expert in medicine. It's beneath me to sell."*

> *"I didn't train in my field for a decade to be a salesperson."*

> *"My work should speak for itself. I shouldn't have to beg people to hire my company."*

And it's no surprise. Americans have attached a negative connotation to the term "selling." For many, it's synonymous with being aggressive and misleading. That's the reason why the phrase "used car salesman" is used as a pejorative, not simply a description of what someone does for a living.

In many small businesses, the owner takes sole responsibility for selling – whether or not she *should.* It's natural: manpower is at a premium and everyone involved in the enterprise wears multiple hats. And those hats come with a variety of challenges.

Solo can be no-go

One of the most common challenges facing seller-doers? They typically don't have a clear sales strategy.

A sales strategy is simply a process, a particular approach and series of activities that you can measure and monitor. But you can't create an effective sales strategy on a whim. A sales strategy requires a series of decisions. You must identify your ideal customer, your unique selling proposition, the geographic area you'll target, and your sales methodology.

It doesn't stop with those decisions. You must also continuously measure to determine whether the sales strategy is working. And when it's *not* working, you need to tweak aspects of it to improve results. For the overloaded business owner, this can be daunting.

Signs that your sales strategy needs some work:

- You don't prospect for new customers often enough or with the right methods.

- You're making phone calls but should be going door to door.

- You might be spending your time on the phone to generate leads when you should have a strong Internet presence.

- You don't have the right sales process to convert browsers to buyers.

Hoping the sale happens

Another challenge facing business-owners-as-reluctant salespeople is finalizing the deal: they don't ask for the sale, they fail to follow up with the prospect to get a decision, or they give up too early.

Fearing rejection, the reluctant seller never brings the prospect to the point of communicating a buying decision. These are the victims of the "big prospect pipeline" delusion, the mistaken idea that potential sales are just around the corner, because they have a large list of prospects who haven't yet said "no."

They don't get training

You've heard the comment, "He's a born salesperson." Don't believe that myth! The best salespeople aren't born; they're *made*. While some people are blessed with traits often found in sales superstars, like optimism and need for achievement, it takes training and persistence to become an effective salesperson. When you have a negative opinion about selling and a self-identity as someone who's "just not a natural salesperson," you're much less likely to invest in training to improve those sales skills.

Out of sight, out of mind

Owners who are too busy "doing" to sell suffer from another revenue reducer: they stop prospecting or don't consistently stay in touch with current customers to get *more* orders. Wrapped up in delivering the work, this owner won't begin pursuing sales again until the revenue stops flowing and the pipeline is dry. It's a cash flow rollercoaster of feast or famine.

Flying blind

When owners are focused on operations output instead of sales, they don't effectively use systems to track their accountability. These owners *feel* busy, but aren't tracking the data to know how many sales conversations they're actually having or what percentage of those turned into clients. This means that they aren't taking action to improve their numbers either.

Now, it's clear that small business owners who are responsible for making sales for their businesses face a series of challenges. But having a sales staff is not problem-free either. For those who employ a salesperson or a sales team, is the path to bigger and better revenues clear?

Nope. It's strewn with a different set of challenges. Let's run through the most common ones that I've seen during my work with hundreds of businesses.

Reluctant sales leader

When small business owners hire their first salesperson, reasonable expectations aren't always clear. Not having sales experience themselves, these owners are uncomfortable stipulating the results they require. After all, is it fair to demand that your employees perform to a standard that you can't match? This doubt can lead the owner to retain an ineffective salesperson for too long, paying a salary for nine months to a year or more with no results.

I saw this play out when a small software company hired its first dedicated salesperson. Ed relocated from Indiana to Michigan to take on the role. He worked for 18 months and made few sales – too few to offset the salary draw that was part of his compensation package. At the end of this period, the owner asked Ed to resign and to pay back a portion of the draw per the employment contract. With no income, Ed couldn't repay the draw, and the owner was faced with pursuing legal action against a plaintiff who couldn't pay. Everyone lost. But here's the relevant business lesson: the magnitude of loss could have been mitigated if the owner had taken action *more quickly* to let Ed go. And Ed might have found a job where he could be successful.

Activity enigma

Owners who aren't comfortable with sales themselves often don't know how to hold their sales staffs accountable, nor do they have effective reporting mechanisms. How many calls should the salesperson make? How many *is* she making? What's a competitive "close rate" for your industry?

When it comes to coaching the salesperson, the owner who's inexperienced in sales simply doesn't have the resources to coach on where to spend time. New prospects? Existing customers? Large prospects that take a longer time to close? Small prospects at a small volume?

Not hiring qualified salespeople

Without sales expertise, it's even a challenge to hire the right *type* of person for the sales you need. Will your sales professional be cold-calling to start a new territory, or growing business within an established base? Those are different efforts requiring different skill sets.

Even if an owner has had successful sales experience, this doesn't automatically transfer to the new salesperson. Owners who've been productive salespeople for their own operations enjoy contacts, relationships, and deep institutional knowledge that can't be simply handed off to the new salesperson.

Another common blunder made by even the most seasoned entrepreneurs is hiring a salesperson based on an "outgoing personality." Big mistake! Being glib in an interview is no determinant of sales ability. In fact, research from Adam Grant, associate professor of management at the Wharton School at the University of Pennsylvania, shows that "the most gregarious salespeople are not the most successful." Grant cites a report in *Scientific American*, "…extroverted salespeople may sometimes be too pushy and turn potential buyers off."[2]

---

[2] [http://www.scientificamerican.com/article.cfm?id=successful-salespeople-have-moderate-temperaments]

Unfortunately, you can't determine sales acumen from just an interview. And the challenge doesn't stop there. Not only do you need to verify whether your candidate has real sales skills, but you must also identify the best match for the type of sales opportunity you already have at your company.

Do you need a "hunter"? These are salespeople who excel at winning new accounts. They thrive on a challenge, but often lose interest once the challenge is won. Great for generating new business, but not so hot for repeat business.

Or is it a "farmer" you seek? In sales jargon, a "farmer" is a salesperson who excels at getting repeat orders and maximizing revenue from existing accounts. Natural nurturers, these people typically aren't the best at winning new clients – they prefer to develop long-term relationships.

I'm my own best example of this sales skill differential (and a warning against basing hiring decisions solely on interviews). Because I'm friendly, outgoing, and personable, it would be a cakewalk for me to get hired in a sales role. However, as someone who doesn't like hearing "no," I'd be successful at developing and sustaining long-term relationships in an existing client base, but terrible at opening a new territory.

Hiring salespeople requires a good job description, great interview questions and, to really ensure success, personality assessments. However, following this recipe takes time, thought, and money. If owners are unclear what to do, they tend to hire the first fast talker who comes their way, usually with poor results.

Let's look at a few more challenges that can plague an entrepreneur when it comes to sales.

Compensation confusion

When it comes to paying their sales staff, small business owners are often befuddled. Salary, straight commission, salary plus commission, bonus? How often? What percentages? It's complicated. Different industries have different compensation norms. But it's something you must get right, because incentive programs can have a huge impact on your bottom line and the growth of your business.

Your magic numbers

When it comes to setting the goals for your sales team (or salesperson), what metrics do you use? Too many business owners target numbers with a shot-in-the-dark methodology, something as non-strategic as "10% more than last year." The trouble is that these leaders haven't determined KPIs (key performance indicators) to help guide their sales teams' activity levels. KPIs, you'll remember, are numbers that are measured to assess the performance of your organization, a specific business unit, or individual employees.

To figure out which KPIs you should track related to sales, look back at your records and determine what has to happen to get a sale in your business. How many leads are required? How many sales calls? What's the average conversion rate (the percentage of prospects who take the next action toward becoming a paid customer)? Can you improve the conversion rate? How much does each customer typically purchase? Can you make that number higher?

Here's a list of sales and marketing sample KPIs to get you thinking about your own operation:

- Sales steps conversion rates
- Conversion rate by salesperson
- Cost per lead
- Cost per sale

- Number of leads by advertising source
- Number of total leads
- Average dollar sale
- Number of transactions per customer
- Dollar product returns
- Length of sales cycle
- Sales by customer type
- Sales by product type
- Sales per day/week/month/season
- Percent of discount sales
- Lost customers

Having a numbers gap (or, ahem, a numbers *vacuum*) is particularly dangerous in situations where the owner has been doing all the sales and then hires a salesperson to take over. Because the owner has been running on "gut feel," he probably hasn't kept track of metrics and can't guide the new salesperson.

Reporting required

Companies with numbers gaps typically suffer from reporting gaps as well. Without solid internal reporting, how can you know if your sales strategy is working? Does the product mix need a tweak? Should you shake up pricing? How about your delivery area – should you expand or contract? If you don't track and evaluate the entire gamut of factors that affect your sales revenue (including product offering, geography, and the sales process itself), you'll never know what needs to be reworked.

Gene is CEO of a company that sells custom testing equipment for automotive companies. No business neophyte, he'd made the *Inc. 500* list of fastest-growing companies in America in the mid-2000s. Just a few years later, he came to me because cash flow was a problem and revenues weren't growing any more.

When I questioned Gene about his company's conversion rates and sales cycle, he confessed that he didn't do much sales reporting. Likewise, he wasn't actually sure about the effectiveness of his salesperson's performance. David, the salesperson, pointed to a large pipeline, promising that the company was on the brink of tremendous sales. With no deadline for closing, those prospects forever remained phantom revenue. Gene couldn't forecast his sales or judge how well David was performing because he had no reporting to give him accurate numbers.

Training is critical

Entrepreneurs who are busy running a company often don't have time to train a new salesperson. In fact, they may not know *how* to train them.

Then there are owners who believe that the salesperson should come into the role fully equipped to hit the ground running. This practice can be dangerous. Leaving new sales staffers to fend for themselves robs them of the opportunity to fully understand your business and to establish the internal relationships – with customer service, operations, finance, etc. – that will help them do their job.

Why It's Broken

A 2006 Gallup poll showed that the public holds an inferior view of the sales profession and rated commissioned salespeople as "dishonest" and "unethical." The survey also revealed that the public thinks of salespeople as fast-talking, pushy, and insincere. As a result, there is, in some industries, a negative stigma attached to being a salesperson.[3]

---

[3] http://www.cob.niu.edu/jsmam/archive/Vol%207%20No%204.pdf

It's natural that a business owner with a negative opinion of sales would shirk those sales duties. But there's a host of other misconceptions that can undermine sales performance in a small business.

If we build it, they will come

Years ago, small business owners didn't need sales strategy. If you were good at what you did, business came to you. With little competition, word of mouth paved the way.

No more. Competition inside and outside the U.S. is on the rise. According to a report from *Global Entrepreneurship Monitor,* there was a 60% increase in entrepreneurship rates in 2011 after a six-year flatline.[4]

This means that there are more businesses competing for your customers' share of wallet.

Sales rollercoaster

Owners get distracted with day-to-day operations. It's easy to put "selling" on the back burner (even more so when you're not comfortable with selling). It's the reason why companies have wild swings in their sales – they focus on selling and they bring in business; then they focus on the production and sales drop; they focus again on sales, and the cycle continues.

Possibility of yes

As long as potential sales opportunities stay in the pipeline, many owners feel good about their prospects, but once they hear that "no," it's frustrating. They have to remove that possible sale from the pipeline report and revenue projections. They also don't want to be

---

[4] http://www.gemconsortium.org/docs/download/2409

"that pushy salesperson" so they may never ask for the sale or make the follow-up calls.

The right sales training

By now, I must have convinced you that salespeople aren't born; they're made through consistent training and development. Easy, right? Wrong. The concept of training brings even more questions and challenges for the small business owner.

Sales is an ever-changing skill. It takes years or even decades to master. Training helps salespeople hone their skills and adapt new techniques in a changing marketplace. But finding the right sales training can be difficult and expensive. The choices can be overwhelming.

You wonder if your sales training should specialize in your industry. Or should it be a fresh, innovative approach that's never been seen in your field? Should you use consultative selling or persuasive selling or some other method? Which will be most effective?

Here are a few of the most popular sales methodologies:

- Action Selling
- CustomerCentric by Michael Bosworth
- Miller-Heiman strategic selling
- Sandler Sales System
- SPIN Selling by Neil Rackham

Each method allows you to get different insights into the sales process for different situations. So if situations vary so greatly, what's the value in using a sales methodology at all? Why not just "wing it"?

The truth is, there's no one-size-fits-all sales formula. The type of sales approach that will be successful in your business depends on what you're selling, the size of the sale, and the type of buyer who purchases your products or services.

No matter what training you choose, using a methodology (or creating your own) allows you to apply a systems approach to the complex interactions that create a sale. You'll be able to document, track, measure, evaluate, and improve your company's success at each stage of the process when you use a system for selling.

Having a sales system will help you attract top sales talent, too. Many salespeople don't like to work for companies that have no proven track record of sales or system for selling. Achievement-oriented by nature, experienced salespeople want to know the rules for "winning."

Compensation

Knowing what to pay employees can be tricky, but figuring out the compensation structure that motivates a salesperson – without making it too difficult or too easy to be successful financially – is particularly complex.

Plus, different things motivate each person. Some will be motivated by money, while others will be motivated by time off, prizes, trophies, etc. It's a balancing act to find a compensation plan that has the broadest appeal.

It often boils down to finding the right balance between base pay and commission. How do you set parameters for performance? How do you measure that performance?

Motivation

Amazon.com boasts more than 38,000 books on motivation in its virtual stacks. That's because motivation is an incredibly complex and nuanced subject. And if motivating *yourself* is a daunting proposition, how about motivating your sales staff? Salespeople get discouraged, especially knowing that – like you – other people's livelihoods depend on their success. How do you lift them up? Is this *your* responsibility? Do you use the carrot approach? The stick? Both?

Remember me?

A major component of a successful sales strategy is keeping in touch with past customers to secure future purchases. It sounds easy, but isn't always simple for every small business.

Some customers don't buy consistently, or the products don't lend themselves to repeat sales. When this is the case, how often should you keep in touch with past customers? There isn't one answer. Again, it requires deliberate decisions and a tested strategy. Roofers, house painters, sellers of enterprise management software systems – customers of these companies may purchase only once a decade. To make it more complicated, you need to consider not only how frequently people want their homes repainted, but also how often they need to hear from you to keep you top of mind so that they can recommend you to friends and family.

Pricing problems sink sales

Ready for more complexity, business owner? Let's talk pricing. How you price the goods or services your small business offers will affect the sales volume of those goods or services. It's an important factor in consumer demand and involves several key elements that require thought, strategy, and research.

If you're busy working the operations side of the business, how can you know what pricing should be? Having a system to review what's going on consistently in your market is vital when it comes to sales, but it's difficult to do. And if you don't have time or salespeople to help to gather the information, it's impossible to keep up, particularly when the market is changing so rapidly. Who has time to research all your competitors? And how do you get the information?

What Will Fix It

The successful CEOs I interviewed had similar attitudes about sales, even when their individual practices differed. Rather than "winging it," each CEO articulated a specific sales strategy governing the organization, continuously tracked results, and adjusted the approach as needed.

One of our Super Owners, Micky, said it best: "We can't wait for things just to get better. We have to make our own luck. We have to determine where things are happening and who has what going on. It's hard work in the trenches. There's no magic in that. It's just consistently doing what you do and doing it well."

Stay in the know

Jim, CEO and co-founder of an automotive parts supplier, is actively involved in the sales process. In the early days of the 10-year-old company, he built a detailed cost model to ensure that all sales were profitable.

When I asked the reasons that his company remained profitable when so many others couldn't, Jim talked about his priorities. "We stayed *very* focused on sales during the downturn," he said. "Now, we review costs daily and measure sales numbers, such as quotes, monthly. As the owner, I approve 100% of the quotes and take accountability for the pricing. We take into account future economics and believe that you have to upsell your company so that you're not just a commodity. If you can't do that, why race to zero?"

Ron, CEO of a five-person vehicle repair business, keeps a sharp eye on sales, too: "We run sales reports daily. If a number's going in the wrong direction, we take action, right then."

Expand when others contract

Strengthening relationships with customers drove another positive outcome for recession survivors: even though budgets were shrinking, they were able to score a bigger piece of the pie as buyers consolidated suppliers in the down economy.

Mitch, founder of a $1.5-million collision repair business, credits reaching out to new markets and trying different distribution methods as key survival strategies. But relationships ruled, too. "We service the heck out of customers," he says.

Hiring by design

When it came to hiring salespeople who produced, the most successful CEOs in my study weren't just lucky. They were deliberate, developing a hiring system that identified highly qualified candidates.

Here are a few of their recommendations:

- **Use a job description that clearly identifies the aptitude required for the job,** what reporting is required, and the sales results you're looking for. Specific phrases let the applicant know what's expected: "open a new territory," "call on existing clients to increase penetration," "prospecting is 80% of the job," and so on. Don't sugarcoat your expectations!

- **Develop a list of interview questions in advance.** To discern the candidate's real traits and skills, it's best to use behavior-based questions. Behavioral-based interviewing means asking questions designed to discover how the interviewee previously acted in specific employment-related situations. It's based on the principle that how you behaved in the past will predict how you will behave in the future. (We'll go much deeper into this topic in Chapter 7, Build an Exceptional Team.)

- **Fish where the fish are.** Give yourself a home-field advantage! Source candidates by advertising in places where you see a lot of ads for sales representatives. If a particular website or job board is known among sales people as the "go to" resource for jobs, then the best candidates are likely already looking there.

Other ideas for finding the best sales candidates:

- **Ask friends and colleagues for referrals.** Your inner circle already knows you and your business. Their recommendations will hold more weight with the candidate and with you.

- **Ask your best performers.** High-achieving go-getters tend to associate with other high-achieving go-getters. Plus, referred employees have higher retention rates and tend to be superior performers.

- **Ask your customers.** Your customers likely work with a host of sales reps. Why not get them to recommend their favorites?

- **Use LinkedIn.** Not only can you advertise directly for salespeople on the site, but you can also find and approach passive candidates (those who aren't actively looking for a job).

- **Use headhunters to save time.** Having trouble finding great candidates? Use a headhunter who specializes in placing salespeople. They can cut down your search time because they'll do a lot of the legwork for you. The right headhunter already has direct experience in your industry. Candidates they source can bring new leads that are already interested in your offerings, as well as new strategies and sales tactics.

Absolutely assess

Once you've sourced a new sales candidate or an entire pool of them, your next step is to dig deeper – to uncover the skills, preferences, and aptitudes you won't learn in an interview.

In a *Wall Street Journal* article, Cheryl Buxton, global managing director of client services for the world's largest executive search firm, Korn/Ferry International Inc., writes:

> *…research has told us that the typical interview – even when conducted by a well-trained professional – can only reveal a person's leadership style (what he or she uses when trying to influence others). Simulation-based assessments, on the other hand, can go a little deeper and determine a person's thinking style, in other words, how he or she makes decisions "when the door is closed and when someone isn't trying to impress someone else."*[5]

Employment assessments are tools as simple as pre-screening questions that ask about work eligibility or as complex as trait measures that assess an applicant's authentic skills, attributes, and motives. Workforce.com, a leading human resources website, says, "Well-designed staffing-assessment tools predict job success with much greater accuracy than traditional employee-selection practices such as résumé reviews and unstructured interviews. This increased accuracy can have a monumental impact on organizational performance and can provide big savings as a result."[6]

---

[5] http://online.wsj.com/article/SB124752560647435361.html
[6] http://www.workforce.com/articles/assessment-tools

Assessments usually fall into three different types of tests: intelligence, personality, and task simulations. The tests and results interpretations can range from $100 to several hundred, but are well worth it if you consider the cost of turnover and lost opportunity that results from bringing on the wrong person. I've known business owners who thought they were hiring a great "closer" only to find they hadn't. Instead, months of productivity were wasted.

Clear expectations, clearly communicated

Once your sales professional is on board, be clear about what you expect, with a thorough job description and internal training that includes your sales process and sales reports, as well as product training.

Have regular meetings to ensure good communication, particularly when salespeople are new to the company. The companies we interviewed had meetings weekly or monthly to discuss progress, challenges, and new ideas.

Our foreign language learning software developers track and use KPIs and financial reports to manage results, and they hold the sales team accountable during weekly meetings. "We know the numbers aren't perfect, but we use them as a benchmark. We're measuring one week to the next, and it helps us focus on the activities that bring revenue, not the ones that make us feel busy," says Jason, summing up one of the factors behind his company's year-over-year growth.

When you're clear about job expectations and measuring results, it's easier to notice when a salesperson *isn't* on track to be successful. And it's easier to take swift action, rather than allowing the situation to drain scarce resources.

Compensate

Employees who contribute directly to a company's profits deserve to be compensated accordingly. But finding the delicate balance between competing interests isn't easy. As an owner, you want the most sales for the least money. Sales professionals want varying degrees of security, together with the highest upside potential.

Our interviewees looked at two factors when determining the sales compensation formula:

1. **The role of the salesperson.** How critical is the salesperson's role in capturing the customer? Is the salesperson answering questions and taking orders, or starting cold and skillfully guiding a prospect through a complex process?

2. **The type of sales.** If you want to incent more new account sales in your business, you'll want to be more aggressive in your pay mix and offer a larger commission. If customer attrition is a problem, make sure that you reward retention success, not only signing new accounts.

Crunch the numbers

For very specific activity requirements, my clients have used the Profit Multiplier Formula (Chapter 2) with individual salespeople to determine the exact number of leads needed to reach individual goals. One client improved sales by 15% within a few months using the formula. This method works because it ties the activities to the end result in clear, undisputable numbers. Each day, each week, the sales professional knows if she's on track to meet her goals.

One client, Tim, even used the Profit Multiplier Formula to make a decision to bring on a new staffer. He crunched the numbers to determine how many sales a new employee would need to make in order to "pay for himself." Armed with this information, Tim felt comfortable expanding his team, and the new sales rep knew what metrics he'd have to hit to keep his place in the organization.

The price is right

Even the most talented sales staff will be stymied when selling mispriced products or services. Earlier in the chapter, I mentioned how challenging the issue of pricing can be if you're not involved in the sales side of the business.

A few of my study participants shared insights into their systems for pricing. While each company varied in the specifics, all their approaches involved certain key factors, such as knowing their target customer, conducting frequent competitive reviews, and positioning between quality and price.

Continuous investment

Our winners shared a common practice for sales: they invest in ongoing training and development. These CEOs know that best practices for sales are always evolving – great books, classes, conferences, and coaches keep skills fresh and effective.

Training can be used as a reward for your best performers so they can continue honing their skills. By lowering employee turnover and increasing productivity, training is one of the smartest investments an employer can make. Successful owners use conferences to allow salespeople from non-competing companies in the same industry to compare notes on how to improve sale efforts.

To get sales, get out

Business owners of companies as diverse as automotive repair centers and restaurants reported that, during the recession, they intensified relationships with clients. These CEOs were leaving the office to meet with clients personally.

Noe, the owner of a Mexican restaurant doing $2 million a year in sales, believes that he runs a "people business." To prove that deeper relationships with customers would protect revenue even during a down economy, he started "running food." In restaurant vernacular, this means that he was delivering plates of food from the kitchen to the customers' tables. Getting physically involved in the transaction gave him an opportunity to inspect quality and speak to the customers. "I believe it makes a difference," he says. "Relationships are important."

You need a sales system

A strategy such as increasing contact with your best customers requires records of sales frequency and profitability per sale. Having good records requires using some sort of tracking system, quite often a customer relationship management (CRM) tool. A CRM is a system that uses technology to manage an organization's interactions with prospects and customers, including sales, marketing, customer service, and technical support.

Popular CRM tools include Salesforce.com, Microsoft Dynamics CRM, ACT! InfusionSoft Small Business CRM, and Netsuite (along with enterprise systems that manage inventory, operations, and customer relations, like SAP and Oracle). CRM systems that can track prospect and customer contacts as they progress through the sales cycle are extremely helpful.

Too many small businesses try to manage this function with spreadsheets, but that's a mistake. It's just too difficult. While an SAP or Oracle installation can cost upwards of a $1 million, most CRMs don't have to be expensive. Some are even free or low-cost, offering broad capabilities for a few hundred dollars a month. At the very least, information is kept in the same place, making it easy to find. And when multiple people are reaching out to the same prospects, it's critical to share that information so you don't look like a company that doesn't have a clue internally.

Keep it simple

Salespeople typically hate spending time on paperwork, so keeping your systems simple is paramount. Time is a salesperson's enemy because it governs how many deals can be closed in a finite period.

And because another sales personality trait is independence, determine how many reports you really need to manage effectively and nix the rest. No one likes to be micro-managed.

The successful sales secrets of recession-defying companies aren't rocket science. A clear sales strategy, strong customer relationships, pursuing market expansion, hiring top talent, measuring all activity, and continuously investing in sales training – none of these are innovative concepts. Yet, during a period when we lost nearly 200,000 small businesses, the top 50 CEOs I interviewed focused on these practices and reaped the results. So can you.

CHAPTER SUMMARY
Embrace Sales

Key Points

Success Code Principle #5: Have a specific sales strategy that includes great salespeople, capturing new markets, and measuring all activity.

- You need a specific sales strategy. This may be difficult if you have no sales experience yourself.

- Don't just hope for sales; ask for them.

- Offer your people the best training you can afford. Great salespeople are *made*, not born.

- Track numbers for all important categories, and take heed of what you learn from them.

- Hire salespeople who are right for the kind of sales you need: hunters or farmers, or both. Sharpen your job descriptions, including a list of needed skills and the assessments you'll use to make your hiring decisions.

- If you want to properly motivate your sales staff, carefully plan how you'll compensate them. Know what each person values as a reward.

- Stay in touch with customers yourself, as much as you can.

- Set a method for reporting and sharing results, through a CRM or other device.

CHAPTER 6
Advance Your Marketing

Most business owners don't have unlimited budgets for marketing. In fact, most have little to no budget. But the right marketing is critical to draw in new prospects, maintain brand image, and where possible, increase market share as competitors go out of business. To do it right, the successful owners I interviewed spent a great deal of time up front – determining the strength of their target markets and re-evaluating their value propositions, making their dollars stretch by using strategic alliances and other relationships in the community, and testing and measuring every strategy for return on investment.

Wish you could improve marketing in your business? You're not alone.

It's a business truth: marketing – communicating the value of your product or service to customers so they buy – is critical to your business survival. You can have the finest product imaginable, but if no one's buying it, your business can't survive.

Business management guru Peter Drucker once said, "Business has only two functions – marketing and innovation."[1]

What's Broken

Most of the businesses I encounter have a problem in their marketing. In fact, that's the most common complaint I hear from business owners. They say, "I just can't seem to get enough clients. I feel like I spend all my time out hustling for business." Or "Business would be great…if it weren't for the customers. They price-shop and complain. It makes me dread going to work."

The right marketing can propel your organization to the top of your industry. The wrong marketing (and yes, having *no* marketing is

---

[1] http://forbes.com/2006/06/30/jack-trout-on-marketing-cx_jt_0703drucker.html

wrong) will leave you scrambling for revenue each month, losing market share, and constantly shrinking your profit margins just to keep the doors open.

It's not getting easier

Email marketing service provider Constant Contact conducted a survey of small business owners to ask how running a business has changed in the last five years. Here's what they found: "Some 59% of decision-makers at small businesses say it's harder to run a business today than it was five years ago."

No surprise there. More than half of respondents in their survey said the economy was the top reason for increased difficulty. The biggest change the group cited – 84% – was "using, or using more, online marketing tools."[2]

Across the span of business history, online marketing is a relatively recent development. But the changes that technology and the Internet have wrought is astonishing.

Online marketing is just one component of the broader whole. Advertising, search engine optimization, email marketing, coupons, networking, direct mail, social media, trade shows, events…it's challenging for marketing experts to keep up with, let alone a business owner who's already playing too many roles.

When your business doesn't have a healthy marketing ROI (return on investment)

What does it look like when a company's marketing ROI falls into the "unhealthy" zone?

---

[2] http://news.constantcontact.com/news/how-running-small-business-has-changed-infographic

You waste precious time and money, only to be disappointed by the lack of prospects in your pipeline. Low numbers of prospects lead business owners to commit acts of desperation – heavy discounting, promising expensive changes to products, stretching the scope of services in order to "win the sale," taking on customers who aren't a good fit, and chasing, chasing, chasing. These desperate acts erode profitability and, worst of all, they erode your confidence in your own abilities.

Right business, wrong customers

Smart business owners pay attention to customer insights, looking for ways to exploit a target market's need with a fantastic product or service. But there's a delicate balance between making business tweaks to better align with customer insights and bouncing from one bad-fit customer to another.

One of the most common mistakes I see among small business owners is not defining their target market clearly or narrowly enough. It's an easy trap to fall into, this belief that everyone is a potential customer. After all, when business isn't robust, it can be scary to think about turning anyone away. The truth is, there are always customers for whom your business – your product or service – is not the right fit.

> Wrong-fit customers are hard to close.
>
> Wrong-fit customers won't spend money.
>
> Wrong-fit customers won't tell their friends about your company.
>
> Wrong-fit customers will consume more customer service resources than they contribute in profit.
>
> Wrong-fit customers will drain your team's energy and your own.

As a business owner, you're better off without them.

Fair weather buyers

The recent daily-deal social couponing craze spurred by consumers looking for bargains highlights how an influx of the wrong customers can actually harm your business.

Coupons aren't a great deal for every business. Certain small businesses have used services such as Groupon or Living Social to "prime the pump," spurring a flow of new customers to their restaurant, retail store, or service business and then crafted that into sustained growth. But most small businesses eventually suffered.

A 2011 article in the news and opinion website, The Daily Beast, cited David Reibstein, marketing professor at the University of Pennsylvania's Wharton School of Business, who warned that daily deal sites could be a negative. He predicted that businesses would suffer and owners "would realize that the coupons aren't a great deal for them." Reibstein pointed out that Groupon's customers are not likely to turn into repeat customers because of their price sensitivity.

This was later proven when marketing researchers tracked three businesses for one year after they offered a social coupon:

> All three companies lost money the month they offered the coupon and will have difficulty earning it back. According to analysis done by the two researchers, V. Kumar and Bharath Rajan, the companies would need 15, 18, and 98 months (almost eight years) to earn back their lost profits. The reason? "The three businesses had difficulty retaining most of the new customers who were attracted to the coupon offers," the two researchers wrote in the *MIT Sloan Management Review*.[3]

No once-and-win

Merchants who defied the odds and have used daily-deal coupons successfully did so because they had a solid strategy for turning those initial visits into repeat customers. Executing a strategy requires marketing consistency.

The poor marketers – the businesses that were crushed by the recession – didn't have a *consistent system or marketing plan*. Marketing isn't a one-time event; it's an ongoing strategy and practice. One standalone tactic, such as placing an ad or starting a Facebook page, isn't enough to create a sustainable flow of revenue.

Revenue *and* profit

Small business owners who ignore marketing typically underperform in both revenue and profit. Topline, these companies just don't have enough sales to drive growth, but lack of marketing also impacts profits by selling to the wrong customer or spending so much on marketing to gain customers that profit margins suffer.

Owners who have no consistent marketing plan also experience cash flow problems because of the revenue roller coaster I mentioned in the chapter on sales. They perform *some* marketing, generate a few prospects, focus all their efforts on closing those prospects, and then perform the work. Once the work is complete, the pipeline is empty. It may take weeks or even months to attract new prospects, convert them, and earn more revenue.

Inventory flux

The feast-or-famine effect makes it tough to control inventory as well. Here's a common scenario: a surge of marketing brings in a flood of customers. You run out of the very items the new customers want most, so you order lots of inventory. And just as suddenly, the initial flood of customers dwindles to a trickle…but now your business is

---

[3] http://www.thedailybeast.com/articles/2012/11/30/why-groupon-and-living-so-cial-are-doomed.html

bloated with a warehouse of excess inventory and no revenue to pay for it.

Starving sales

Lack of marketing success can impact your sales by creating a revolving door of salespeople. It's a fact – salespeople like making sales. Many don't enjoy prospecting, so if they don't have enough leads to close and make commissions, they get discouraged.

Marketing and sales operates best as a continuum: marketing creates awareness and interest in your company, your products and services, and nurtures prospects until they are ready to be closed by sales. Depending on how your business operates and what you're selling, this entire process from awareness to purchase could take place in five minutes, or it could take 12 months or more.

First impressions last

Marketing done poorly can make your business appear unprofessional, which can leave a lasting impression on your prospects. I get it – you don't have a big budget to spend on high-end commercials or fancy graphics. Bootstrapping is more than an in-vogue business term. It's a necessary way of life.

Have you ever received a postcard or an email riddled with spelling and grammar errors and poor design? How did the experience influence your perception of that business? Unprofessional marketing not only makes it harder to convince prospects to buy from you, but it can actually harm your business.

Case in point: email marketing can be a powerful tool for lots of different businesses. It seems simple, right? Buy a list, dash off a bit of text announcing your next sale, push Send, and start counting your money.

Wrong. Email messages with bad copy are likely to be deleted, unread. Worse, certain words in the subject line or body of the message may trigger spam filters and then the Internet service provider won't deliver the email. And if the email recipients haven't given permission, your business could be identified as a spammer, rendering you unable to send or receive emails. Ouch. Saving a few hundred dollars by doing it yourself could cost you *thousands* if you don't know the laws and best practices.

Business as bland

A marketing challenge that constantly trips up small business owners is how to stand out in a crowded marketplace. While it's a struggle for any sector, this particularly plagues professional service providers. For restaurants and retail businesses, the merchandise, the location, and the physical surroundings create some of the differentiators.

But pick up a brochure or scan the website of a service provider and I'll wager that you can't differentiate most from their competitors. They look the same. They sound the same. How many businesses tout themselves as "the area's premier provider of (insert service)." Or boast, "We strive to offer exceptional customer service. Our knowledgeable staff members are here to fulfill all your (whatever) needs."

Here's an old trick to see if your company's marketing is conveying what's different about your company. Take two similar marketing pieces, one from your company and one from a competitor (it could be your website message or brochures.) Black out the names and logos, and ask a friend to tell you which one describes your company. You might be shocked at what you learn.

Why It's Broken

The very premise of marketing seems confusing. It can be hard to define – what's marketing, what's sales, and how do they fit together? Many owners aren't comfortable with it and haven't taken the time to study even the fundamentals.

Business owners whose zone of genius revolves around numbers often seem terrified of marketing. For a few clients I've worked with, the aversion is so extreme that they almost have a phobia about it. But that fear can't be indulged. Whether small business owners learn to love (okay, *tolerate*) marketing or outsource it strategically, it's the key to sustainable growth.

Businesses with poor or nonexistent marketing practices suffer in a variety of ways. Let's look at the reasons.

It feels like a moving target

While the fundamentals of marketing haven't changed, how they're executed has shifted remarkably. With the advent of the Internet and now mobile devices, there are so many more ways to reach prospects and promote than ever before. Ten years ago, Facebook was only an idea in Mark Zuckerberg's dorm room. YouTube didn't exist. Google Adwords, Groupon, Yelp? Nope. And those represent just a slice of the online marketing world.

But even more fundamental challenges exist than the rapidly changing tools.

DIY danger

Business owners tend to be self-sufficient types – do-it-yourselfers. That "git 'er done" attitude is often a boon in business, but when it comes to marketing, taking on the entire function yourself may be a bad idea for three reasons:

1. "Unconscious incompetence," or "you don't know what you don't know." Reading a few articles in your industry

trade magazine or attending a marketing workshop aren't enough to give you the foundational principles you need to make sound decisions. You could spend $15,000 on a website when you should focus on hosting events. Or you might spend all your time on social media instead of content marketing and improving search engine optimization, so customers find your website when searching for a solution.

2. It's hard to be objective. Your business is your baby. You can't see your company, your products and services, with an unbiased perspective. And that makes it tricky to market effectively.

3. The hallmark of good marketing is ROI (return on investment.) That means that you have to invest, whether it's through your own time or paying an outside professional. Consider the highest and best use of your time. Is it marketing or other business activities?

My customer is men and women, 0-65

One of the most fundamental marketing challenges is identifying the right target market. When business owners struggle to identify their target customers, they don't know *where* they should be marketing or *how* to reach their prospects. As a result, they use a scatter-shot approach and market everywhere…or nowhere.

Most business owners believe that they are best served by appealing as broadly as possible, but the truth is really the opposite. *Narrowing* your focus to a particular demographic or geographic piece of the market is a more effective use of your marketing resources – money and time. Only when you can effectively reach a specific group and convince them that your product or service is perfect for them can you overcome the "noise." From a customer's point of view, when a product or service isn't remarkably different from others in the marketplace, he or she will base the decision on one attribute: price.

Greg Head, founder and CEO of New Avenue, a strategic marketing firm, contends that not everyone can be your customer. "Focus requires exclusion," he says. "If you're selling everything, you actually mean nothing in the marketplace. Exclusion is fundamental to target markets."[4]

If marketing wisdom dictates that you must narrow your target market to win business, why do so few businesses take this step?

Fear.

I teach an effective networking class for business owners, sponsored by my local Chamber of Commerce. Of all my material, "Identifying a Specific Target Market" is the piece that the participants resist most strongly. They're terrified of turning away business. And the more desperate they are to grow, the stronger the fear.

Remarkably unremarkable

Another thing that plagues small business owners when it comes to marketing – they don't know how to differentiate themselves from their competitors. They aren't clear on their company's unique selling proposition, or USP.

When you're deep in the weeds, it's hard to see the blades of grass. The most common mistake is making the same generic claims that other businesses do: great customer service, years in business. Saying that you have great customer service isn't unique or differentiating. Today's consumer considers being responsive to customers a business

---

[4] http://www.inc.com/guides/201104/how-to-narrow-your-target-market.html

standard. If your customer service is unique, *what is it specifically that sets you apart?*

To stand out, you must do something remarkable. Zappos is an often-used example of remarkable customer service, with good reason. The online shoe retailer entered a commodity-based market and used customer service as a true USP. To do so, they did things that other companies wouldn't, such as giving free shipping on returns as well as deliveries, and hiring customer service agents who love to serve others and empowering them to take action to please customers (even when it costs money), rather than just follow a script.

Your business's USP could be the experience you create for your customers, or how you operate your business. Kinko's combines a unique experience with remarkable operations. Founder Paul Orfalea grew Kinko's from a one-man operation in 1970, eventually selling his interest to a Wall Street buyout firm for $116 million in 2003. He differentiated Kinko's from other copy service providers by making his stores a soothing sanctuary for stressed-out business people. "We weren't so much making copies as we were assuaging anxiety," Orfalea wrote in his biography. He borrowed ideas from convenience stores (staying open 24 hours a day, which increased per-customer visits) and McDonald's (efficient workspace design) to keep his growing chain's profits high, even in a commodity industry (Business Brilliant, 2013).

Knee-jerk marketing

When struggling small business owners finally turn to marketing, it's often a singular and reactionary act: "Sales are down by 40%! Quick, run a coupon in the local newspaper."

Too often, these owners treat each marketing effort – advertisement, sponsorship, direct mailing, trade show – as a one-off event. They don't strategize or set goals *before* a campaign or event to get the most out of it. They lack a long-term plan. Failing to grasp the lifetime value concept, these are the same owners who focus on the expense of marketing, but are oblivious to the lifetime value of one new customer. The catch-22 is that owners who view marketing as an expense black hole rarely do enough of it to experience results.

Great, it's working! Let's change it!

Marketing is one place where change is not always good. But there are business owners who will change a successful marketing tactic or strategy just because they're bored with it. It's human nature to crave a little variety, but marketing is one area where you should apply the motto, "If it ain't broke, don't fix it."

Father-daughter marketing strategists Al Ries and Laura Ries lament the fatal flaw of much advertising – small business and big brand alike – in their book, *The Fall of Advertising & The Rise of PR* (HarperBusiness, 2004).

The Rieses contend that most advertising fails because it's not actionable, not measurable and, too often, it's purely a creative endeavor, not a business-building workhorse. Citing clever advertising campaigns that generated tremendous buzz while sales actually declined, the authors explain that advertising is too often striving for creativity or novelty instead of clearly articulating a value proposition and motivating a prospect to take a specific, measurable action.

And it gets worse. Not only does most advertising fail to do its job of bringing in new purchasers, but when ads *do* work, the client (or the agency) stops using them in favor of something newer or fresher. There's a natural reaction as the owner of the company to grow weary of your own promotions. After all, you're paying closer attention than any other person in the world! But your perspective is not the same as those of your prospects. They may be just getting around to noticing the ad and taking action on it when you change it.

I've seen this with my own clients. Years ago, I asked the manager of a financial planning firm about successful marketing efforts in his business. He shared that his firm had hosted a series of dinners where their clients invited guests to have their financial planning questions answered in a casual, intimate setting. The firm scored a bevy of new clients from the dinners. In fact, he admitted that it was the most successful marketing activity they had executed, but they had stopped doing it. When I asked him why, he laughed and said, "Pretty dumb, but I think we just got bored with it and wanted to try something new."

At the opposite end of the advertising spectrum are those business owners who don't have a clue if their advertising is working but continue to run the same ads because they "don't want to deal with it." Often, these ads tend to be what are called "image" ads, used for branding. They include the company name, logo, and perhaps a tagline, but no call to action. They require no direct response. The company is running the ads just to "get our name out there."

Really? Even with limited resources, this works for you? I believe that as a small business, you should spend most of your marketing budget on the *foundation* – marketing that directly drives action. When you can afford to, you can move up the pyramid to branding or image-type ads.

Follow up failures

Every business has holes – gaps in its systems where opportunities escape and resources are wasted. In prosperous economic times, many businesses don't seem nearly as concerned with slipshod systems that fail to capitalize on revenue opportunities. But those businesses aren't serious about growing.

Even now, barely following the recession, companies continue to throw away thousands of dollars on exhibitor fees, pricey booths, and hotel and staff costs to attend trade shows. And then they don't follow up! Nearly 80% of tradeshow leads are never contacted. I've seen the same phenomenon among business owners I coach. They run a successful marketing campaign that generates leads, but then fail to follow up on those prospects.

While it might seem ludicrous, it's easy to understand how this happens. Tradeshow participants, after being out of the office for several days, get busy unearthing their desks from the work that piled up. Often, there's no plan for follow-up, so that stack of business cards that you paid $4,000 to acquire gets shoved to the back of a desk drawer until it's "too late."

Penny-wise, pound-foolish

Certain owners – particularly those who don't understand marketing – think marketing is a waste of money, so they just don't do it. It makes sense, doesn't it? When you view something as an expense, you try to reduce it as much as possible. That's why so many business owners slashed their marketing budgets during the recession.

Reactionary austerity isn't necessary when you know what works. Having the data to know the return on investment you get from your marketing efforts gives you confidence to spend where it counts.

I'm doing a lot of marketing. Where's the business?

There's a faction of business owners who confuse activity with results. They point to spending as though it should guarantee revenue: "We're running these ads every single week."

In a similar vein, some entrepreneurs have "marketing attention deficit disorder." They jump on the newest advertising method or marketing idea whether or not it makes sense for their industry and audience.

Take social media. Even though Pinterest is one of the fastest-growing social networks and one of the most visited websites in the world (at the time of this writing), it's not the best marketing vehicle for some businesses because of its heavily female audience. For others, a great Pinterest strategy could lead to high ROI.

Go pro

Business owners who don't understand marketing may not value marketing acumen as a legitimate skill set that's as valuable as other business skills like finance. They don't recognize that marketing is sophisticated, nuanced, and takes time to learn. A skeptic won't invest in an experienced professional marketer.

I've seen this trajectory in many professional service firms. At the company's start, the principals of the firm rely on personal relationships to generate business. Unfortunately, that's where some of them stay. These firms' marketing plans consist of golf outings, donating to political campaigns, and wining and dining.

Because these firm principals don't value marketing, they promote a talented administrative assistant to the title of "marketing coordinator." Her role is typically to create PowerPoint slide decks and register foursomes for golf tournaments. No strategy.

Relying only on personal selling can seriously stem a company's growth because it's too expensive to scale.

It always takes longer than you think

A common syndrome plaguing small business owners is underestimating the amount of time a project will take. Marketing is no different. Eternal optimists, entrepreneurs gloss over the challenges that will inevitably arise.

Let's say that you want to send a postcard campaign promoting a holiday special next month. It sounds like a quick-and-dirty task, right? Something that can be turned around in just a day or so? Here's the reality:

1. You or someone else has to write the copy (the words).

2. Then you have to approve the copy. Sometimes multiple people or departments weigh in on the copy and offer more ideas about what should be included. You'll have to decide whether to incorporate all those helpful suggestions. And to wait on the one or two employees who don't respond quickly but want to be included in giving feedback.

3. Next, you need a design. (And believe me, *everyone* will have an opinion on design. Unfortunately, trying to please everyone is *the hallmark* of bad design.)

4. When you look at your mailing list, you realize that it hasn't been updated in several years. Of the 3,000 names on the list, only about 500 are good prospects. The trouble is, you don't know which of the 3,000 are the solid prospects. You assign someone on your team to update the database, but that's on top of his regular duties, so it takes weeks to finish.

5. When you get the postcards back from the printer, you see that the in-house amateur designer didn't notice that an "s" was cut off, making your clever call to action, sound, well, *stupid*. You fix it and reorder the cards.

6. To save money, you ask your teenaged daughter to address and stamp the cards instead of paying extra to have the printer perform that task. She leaves them in her car for a few days until you ask about the status.

Your "quick-and-dirty" marketing project is now going out three weeks later than you intended. Let's hope that holiday hasn't passed!

When considering doing it yourself as a business owner, you have to factor the value of your own time into the decision. If you noticed how you spent your time each day and applied a dollar value to those activities, you might be surprised at the expense. And every minute that you spend fumbling an activity that isn't your genius work robs time you should be spending on high-value tasks.

Mad Men on the loose

A lack of marketing sophistication can lead business owners to trust advertising salespeople who are operating outside their best interests. Don't get me wrong – most advertising sales representatives are ethical, value-driven professionals. But a few aren't. Because much of an advertising sales representative's compensation is based on commission from ad sales, those bad apples will cajole, coerce, and mislead owners into spending large piles of cash on advertising that's ineffective.

Networking nerves

Some of the more introverted business owners – those who relish numbers rather than the people side – view networking as a punishment. Or a task to delegate to the "sales guy or gal" in the business.

Networking gets a bad rap, often because there are so many people who are just plain doing it wrong. From the pushy self-promoter to the shifty-eyed "bigger fish" seeker, aggressive networkers are often people you want to avoid, not embrace.

Authentic networking is different. It's about getting to know people, spending time out of your office and in the company of potential clients and strategic partners.

What Will Fix It

During the time that I conducted my study, I noticed common threads among the businesses that were holding steady or even growing during the recession. There was a strong focus on marketing. Not necessarily spending large amounts, but having a healthy respect for the practice of marketing and strong discipline concerning its use.

While the losers of the recession hewed marketing budgets to the bone or blew major sums on desperate attempts to buy new customers, savvy owners spent time evaluating the strength of their target markets and honing their value propositions. They diversified, retrenched relationships, and tracked every activity to know their marketing return on investment.

Let's dig deeper into their winning habits.

Know your target market

Our entrepreneurial winners were very clear (or quickly got that way) on who their best customer was and what made that person tick. They either hired someone to do the research or made an effort to connect with their customer base to identify the common characteristics of great customers. Who qualifies as a "great" customer? One that's profitable, purchases over and over, and is easy to work with.

Super Owner Tom credits much of his organizational success to his intimate knowledge of his customer. "First, you have to know who your customer is," he says. "Once you know that, you have to figure out what's preventing them from fulfilling their goals. If you offer a solution to meet that need, you can then partner with them in success."

Tom says that research plays a big role in knowing his customer's challenges: "To know your customers' problems, you have to read the magazines they read, join the associations they belong to, and communicate with vendors and suppliers they use. Once you've done that research, you'll know the challenges they're facing."

Does it work? You bet it does. Tom says, "Our customers tell us, 'Your ability to understand what my challenges are and to develop solutions that help me to be successful set you apart from the other companies that do the same work you do.'"

One of our other successful entrepreneurs, Scott, decided his high-tech company couldn't be "everything to everybody" and had a complete willingness to walk away from prospects that didn't fit their profile.

Who are you?

During my interviews, I noticed an interesting phenomenon. The CEOs of the most successful businesses had the most granular knowledge of their customers. They not only knew who their customers were, they knew what appealed to them and why they bought.

Marketing professionals refer to these people markers as *demographics* and *psychographics.*

Demographics describe characteristics of populations, such as sex, race, age, income level, education level, and employment. It's "who" people are: a 37-year-old female African-American computer programmer making $92,000 per year who lives in Reston, Virginia.

Psychographics describe a person's values, attitudes, beliefs, emotions, opinions, and lifestyle. Marketers sometimes refer to these attributes as activity, interest, and opinions (or AIO). It's "why" we do what we do.

The most successful marketing involves selling something people want to the people who want it. When you know your customers' demographics (who they are), you know where to find more of them. And when you know their psychographics (why they buy), you know how to design your product or service and marketing to appeal to them.

Identifying your target audience enables you to determine how much demand exists for your product or service, modify your product or service to better meet customers' specific needs, and design a marketing campaign that speaks to the right people, using the tone and language most likely to appeal to them.

Here's a simple three-step process to identify your target customers:

1. **Create a customer profile.** Look through your customer records and ask your staff about your best customers. What characteristics did they share?

   Denise, owner of a promotional products company, did exactly that by gathering data and information on current customers to help her understand the potential of her target market.

2. **Conduct market research.** With a mix of primary research (research you conduct yourself) and secondary (research conducted by others), you can uncover the best avenues to reach more buyers like your best customers.

3. **Reevaluate your products and services and your marketing.** What can you adjust to make your product more appealing? Do you need to tweak the language you use in your marketing? Should you change your marketing mix – shift resources from trade shows to

search engine optimization so customers find your
business on the web?

Here are few tools and resources to help you find and analyze your
target market:

- **U.S. Census Bureau** is chock-full of information by state,
  city, age, business, geography, and more. That's where
  you'll find data from the most recent Economic Census,
  the U.S. Government's official five-year measure of
  American business and the economy.

- **Google Analytics** is a free service offered by Google that
  tracks and reports visitors to your website, how they got
  there (search words, links from another site), the amount
  of time spent on your site, conversions, and more.

- **Facebook and YouTube Insights.** Both of these services
  include data about who's interacting with your page
  or channel including likes, number of fans, daily
  users, growth in new fans, demographics, and media
  consumption.

- **Survey sites like SurveyMonkey.com.** Getting answers
  straight from your customers can dig up marketing gold.
  Keep surveys short – a few simple questions – and you'll
  home in on your customers' likes and dislikes.

Focus on your strengths

Whenever possible, our top-performing business owners hired out
their marketing. Except for those few for whom marketing is an innate
talent, the owners recognized that they can't be good at all things,
so they found a resource within their budget and got the job done.
Sherman, CEO of a waste management company and one of our Super
Owners, chose to use an outside company for his public relations,
website, and overall marketing, and reaped the success of their efforts

while many of his competitors were struggling.

Most of the business owners I researched were consistently tweaking their marketing strategies to improve results. What's more, none of them stopped marketing during the recession. They may have kept a sharper eye on the budget, but they didn't stop.

Measure and measure

The best-performing companies in my study shared a trait: they were good at measuring most of their marketing efforts. I can't claim that they were perfect, but they did recognize the importance of tracking strategies, activities, and results, especially when money was tight.

Orthopedic practice leader, Dr. Farjo, doesn't believe in unplanned spending. "Don't spend money on advertising without clear ROI." That's seconded by Paul, CEO of a payroll company, who says, "We are very cautious about ROI. We want to make sure all of our marketing efforts can deliver."

Clear ROI requires tracking your marketing efforts and results. It's no coincidence that the highest-performing companies were also those that tracked and measured their critical activities, including marketing. Diane, owner of a home medical supply company, said, "We're rebranding and turning up the advertising budget, but you can be sure we'll be measuring ROI."

Let's look at a marketing strategy driven by investment marketing and lifetime customer value:

> Jay owns a heating and cooling business. His company offers a free furnace inspection to gain new customers. He knows by offering this service for free, he'll invest $60 or more for gasoline, his technician's time, and his office manager's time in scheduling the appointments. Jay also knows that the average customer on

his "Peace of Mind" plan (two maintenance visits per year, plus a guaranteed response time on emergency visits) stays with his company for eight years and generates nearly $7,000 in business. Jay feels confident in making the investment in this marketing effort because he carefully tracked his results. He knows how many prospective clients take advantage of the free inspection and what percentage then join the Peace of Mind plan. He can calculate the return on each dollar invested in this marketing strategy.

Create a budget and a plan

The key to avoiding chaotic marketing and poor results is to create a plan and a budget. But setting a marketing and advertising budget is a daunting challenge for many small business owners because of the many ways to approach the task. Using a percentage of your total sales is one of the most popular methods of budgeting because it allows your marketing spending to fluctuate as your company grows. In the real world, however, marketing and ad budgets vary dramatically based on industry, amount of competition, profit margins, and affordability.

The U.S. Small Business Administration recommends spending 7% to 8% of your gross revenue for marketing and advertising if you're doing less than $5 million a year in sales and your net profit margin, after all expenses, is between 10% and 12%.[5]

In 2010, the Chief Marketing Officers Council conducted a survey of its 6,000 members to measure marketing spending across a variety of industries. The survey results revealed that 58% spent less than 4% of gross revenue, 16% spent around 6% of gross revenue, 23% spent more

[5] http://www.sba.gov/community/blogs/community-blogs/small-business-cents/how-set-marketing-budget-fits-your-business-goa

than 6%, and 2% surveyed spent more than 20%.[6]

Outsourcing can upgrade your brand

Having Microsoft Publisher on your computer doesn't make you a graphic designer. I highly recommend paying someone to provide artwork whenever possible so that your marketing materials look professional.

Here are two low-cost approaches:

1. **Hire a local freelancer.** Ask your network and fellow small business owners to recommend freelance designers or marketers. Many of these will be talented students or employed graphic artists who moonlight. Review their portfolios and client references. Talk to these artists to see if working together would be a good fit. Then give the freelancer a small project to test the person's design and communication skills.

2. **Use a freelancer exchange site like elance.com, freelance.com, guru.com, 99designs.com, or behance. com.** These sites serve as a marketplace for hiring designers and others whose work doesn't require them to be in your office or on your payroll. When you're working with virtual contractors, be articulate and decisive in describing your project and the results you want. Again, follow the same vetting process. The most popular sites protect the freelancer and the buyer with features like online portfolios, freelancer ratings, buyer feedback and reviews, and escrow services for payments.

---

[6] sba.gov/community/blogs/community-blogs/small-business-cents/how-set-marketing-budget-fits-your-business-goa

Do sweat the small stuff

Don't forget that marketing is your entire image. Don't ignore the small bits – your location, clothing, image, logo, level of customer service, all printed pieces (including your business cards), the way you answer your phone, etc. Potential customers won't be convinced of your staff's extraordinary attention to detail if you've got four-foot-tall weeds growing in front of your building.

Here's an example: Mike, owner of a heating and cooling company, realized that answering the phone was a customer touchpoint, so he replaced the company's receptionist with someone better equipped to represent the company to new prospects.

Advertiser beware

Before you commit to any particular marketing tactic, carefully research the companies you will use. For instance, if you're going to advertise on a radio station or in a publication, find out who they reach. Don't be swayed by a huge number of readers or listeners (often called "audience reach"). Instead, dig deep into the demographics of the audience. If it isn't your target market, you'll be wasting your time.

Magazines and newspapers have circulation audits that break down the readership by age, occupation, income level, purchasing authority and other factors. Radio stations have similar listening audience data.

Top-of-mind marketing

John, the owner of a million-dollar floor covering business, believes that creating a strong bond with loyal customers kept his business afloat during the recession. One of his favorite tactics is to send birthday cards with special discount offers to top customers. He uses a service called Send Out Cards, which allows the office manager to upload a customer spreadsheet. Send Out Cards automatically prints and mails the cards to customers on their birthdays.

Salon owner Angela credits her strong community presence with helping her $2-million business survive the recession. She says that she can correlate revenues with the time she spends in the community: "I network through people in the community, the connectors. Our salons sponsor several charities every year, and we participate in a popular fashion show. Being involved keeps my salon top of mind."

Free marketing tools or huge time-sucks?

Because social media is the current latest trend in marketing, some business owners have jumped in with both feet.

My advice? Be cautiously open-minded. On the positive side, social media tools like Facebook, Twitter, LinkedIn, and YouTube offer opportunities to reach your consumer directly. Conversely, if not done correctly, they can be a huge waste of time.

Remember the Dollar Shave Club video I mentioned in Chapter 4? The one that racked up over 11 million views of its sales video on YouTube and cost just $4,300 to make? That's a true social media success story. And here's an important reality check – that kind of out-of-this-world marketing ROI is *extremely rare*. The Dollar Shave Club video is the result of a clever script, a comedy improv-trained CEO, a unique selling proposition, and a fearless desire to stand out in a crowded marketplace.

Will some potential customers be offended by the cheeky video? Oh, yes! (Come on – the video title is "Our Blades are F***Ing Great." That's automatically going to alienate a portion of the potential razor-buying market.) But the bold stance and easy-to-convey business proposition – a subscription service that delivers razors to your home for as little as $2 month – appealed to enough customers to generate 12,000 orders in the first *48 hours* of the video launch.

Know that you don't have to be everywhere on the Internet. Just be in the few places where your target market is likely to participate.

Here are a few more tips:

- **Be personal.** Too many businesses use just the company logo as their social media image. Noooooo! Your potential customers don't want to tweet with a logo or be "friends" with a logo. Use a professional, friendly picture of your face (and definitely not a blurry photo taken at an event). High-profile representatives of large consumer brands, such as Scott Monty, global head of social media for Ford Motor Company, uses a headshot with his company's logo on the image to reinforce the corporate connection.

- **Pick one platform to dominate.** Take on too many social media platforms at once, and you'll burn yourself out. Pick the one most used by your customers and focus your limited time there.

- **Complete your profile.** Twitter, Facebook, YouTube, LinkedIn, and the scads of other social media sites all allow viewers to know a bit about you. Use the opportunity to create a human connection! If you set up a profile on one of these platforms, make it complete. Don't stop at just a photo and bio – give people a little insight into your professional and personal interests. It helps others to connect with you *and* your business.

- **Post consistently.** There's nothing worse than a blog that hasn't been updated in six months or a Twitter feed gone silent. Can you believe customer service promises or claims of extraordinary attention to detail from a company whose Facebook page is a dead zone? If you're going to participate, make a commitment. Determine

how frequently you'll post and schedule time to do
so. Make it easier by creating an editorial calendar – a
schedule of topics and posting frequency for a specific
period of time, usually one quarter, six months, or a year.

Creating a healthy ROI doesn't require copious spending, flashy
advertising, or becoming an Internet sensation. By zeroing in on
your target customer, identifying your company's value proposition,
planning your marketing strategy, and tracking results, your business
can thrive in any economy.

CHAPTER SUMMARY
Advance Your Marketing

Key Points

Success Code, Principle #6: Create a healthy marketing ROI.

- The right marketing is critical to draw in new prospects, maintain brand image, and increase market share.

- The right marketing can propel your organization to the top of your industry. The wrong marketing will leave you scrambling for revenue, losing market share, and constantly shrinking your profit margins.

- Smart business owners pay attention to characteristics defining their target customers so they can exploit those needs with their product or service.

- Lack of marketing success can impact your sales by creating a revolving door of salespeople, lead to poor control of inventory, and affect growth negatively.

- It's best to hire a professional to design your marketing. Marketing done poorly can make your business appear unprofessional, which can leave a lasting impression on your prospects.

- One of the most fundamental marketing challenges is identifying the right target market. Know where you should be marketing and how to reach their prospects.

- Most business owners believe that they are best served by appealing as broadly as possible, but the truth is really the opposite.

- The most common mistake is making the same generic claims that other businesses do. Set your business apart from your competitors.

- Keep your marketing message fresh. Don't be afraid to change it from time to time.

- If you make a marketing investment, such a trade show, follow up on leads.

- Savvy business owners evaluate the strength of their target markets and hone their value propositions.

- Know your target market and work specifically on those customers.

- Create a budget and a plan, and track your efforts.

- Use social networking, but keep it updated and frequent.

CHAPTER 7

Build an Exceptional Team

Building a happy, highly productive team is critical to the growth of a company, but it's one of the areas where many owners fail to excel. The owners of our successful companies realize that, to sustain momentum and keep moving forward, they must create an employee-centered culture (it starts at the top). Team members must be hired based on talent and then given clear expectations and feedback on their productivity, both through coaching and positive reinforcement. Sound easy? It's not.

Struggling owners typically underestimate the power of having the right culture. They hire the wrong people for the wrong reasons, mismanage or micro-manage them, then overreact or ignore the outcomes, whether good or bad. To survive poor economic conditions and thrive in good ones, our owners knew they must be disciplined to consistently put time and attention into communication, accountability, and building relationships.

Building a great team doesn't stop at the walls of your building. The business owners who capitalized on team culture also sought external vendors and service providers who acted as partners, not just order takers.

What's Broken

Even leaders like Henry Ford, who revolutionized industry and the way that we live, struggled with the human resource aspect of business. Ford's lament, "Why is it every time I ask for a pair of hands, they come with a brain attached?" may be legend, but it captures the challenge so many small business owners feel. The art of managing people is something you can't learn through courses alone. It's a skill honed through trial and error.

Business owners who pursued entrepreneurship for the love of practicing their profession or skill can feel betrayed by the burden of managing human capital. Why can't people just do what needs to be done? Why do they need time and attention and ego-stroking in order to do a job?

Even entrepreneurs who enjoy the camaraderie and increased horsepower of having a team sometimes fall victim to human resource management mistakes. Let's examine the warning signs of an ineffective team.

Hands-off management

Certain personality types are more comfortable keeping their employees at a distance. Hoping to avoid uncomfortable interactions and additional stressors, the hands-off owner always lets employees "work it out" themselves. Not a good idea.

Hiding out in your office or keeping yourself buried in work to avoid those pesky people problems will only exacerbate the situation. Your role as the company leader is to facilitate and orchestrate – not hibernate.

Indifference kills teams

Research from the Kellogg School of Management at Northwestern University shows that you must sincerely care about your team if you want to be an effective leader. "Pushing people to do more, while also showing that you care about them, is the great balancing act every leader faces," says Professor J. Keith Murnighan.[1]

Owners who don't care about the people who work for them on a personal level aren't able to spark that desire to strive among their

---

[1] http://www.theglobeandmail.com/report-on-business/careers/the-hands-off-approach-to-leadership/article4480738/

employees. Instead, staffers view these impersonal owners as greedy and self-serving.

What are we fighting for?

During challenging economic conditions, small business owners may contribute even more of their own efforts to their business, but without a team effort behind them, the impact of one individual is limited.

A 2009 *Harvard Business Review* article reported on a study conducted among tens of thousands of working people around the world that showed being forward-looking, "envisioning exciting possibilities and enlisting others in a shared view of the future…is the attribute that most distinguishes leaders from non-leaders."

A whopping 72% of respondents wanted this quality in a leader. However, it's not easy to come by. According to the study, only 3% of the typical business leader's time is spent envisioning and enlisting.[2]

Clarity breeds commitment

When employers aren't clear on their own vision for the company, they can't convey it to their team. This makes it impossible to "rally the troops." Howard Schultz, founder of Starbucks, knows this. "People want to be part of something larger than themselves. They want to be part of something they're really proud of, that they'll fight for, sacrifice for, that they trust."[3]

Without a clear vision, clearly conveyed, your employees don't know the ground rules. Vague company visions touting desires to be the

---

[2] http://hbr.org/2009/01/to-lead-create-a-shared-vision/ar/1
[3] wilsonlearning.com/wlindia/blog/post/want_successful_change_management_get_employee_buy_in1

premier provider of a service or product don't give employees specificity or inspiration.

When you haven't defined what the company stands for and stands against, what you will do and what you won't do, you can't identify the key actions that you need to take and or what success looks like. Your employees don't know what decisions to make or what actions to take. So they'll wait until you tell them exactly what to do. Every step of the way.

Breathing? You'll do

Business owners without a clear vision for their companies typically make hiring mistakes. When you don't know what you want your company to look like in three years, or 10 years, you can't know exactly *who* you'll need on your team to help you achieve the vision.

Instead, these owners bring on team members who can't do their job because they aren't capable. It sounds silly – why would a business owner ever hire an employee who wasn't qualified? It happens *much* more often than you'd think.

Here's a common scenario among small business owners I encounter. The business is growing, but rather than continuously look for new members to flesh out team capabilities, the owners wait until orders are flying in, work is piling up, and stretched staffers are screaming. Now, in a rush to add capacity, the owner or manager hires the first "warm body" who crosses his path. Disaster.

In some of the worst instances, the owner or manager hires a friend or family member. Typically, this is someone in the business owner's circle who happens to be available at the time of need. It seems like a win-win, right? The owner gets additional staff, and the friend gets a job. Unfortunately, it rarely works.

Hiring friends (especially without proper vetting) brings an extra volume of problems. No matter how objective you feel you are, friendship blurs the line between working and personal relationships. Fellow employees will perceive favoritism, even where it doesn't exist. And what about performance? If your buddy, neighbor, or cousin isn't pulling his weight, you'll find it hard to give honest feedback.

Snowed by great interviewees

Without that clear vision for your company and a sharp understanding of the roles and skills you need to execute it, you'll commit another common hiring mistake: falling for a fabulous interviewee. Candidates with charismatic, outgoing personalities make interviewing a pleasure (especially when conducting interviews isn't your strong suit). And that enjoyment can distract you from asking the hard questions to determine whether the person who's wowing you verbally can actually do the job you need done.

In the chapter on sales, I mentioned that because I'm personable and outgoing, I could interview and win most any sales position…even though certain types of sales are not my strength. Most small business owners simply don't dig deep enough to know whether the candidate is a great performer or just a great interviewee.

Team dysfunction

Rigorous hiring and selection processes can help avoid some of the worst offenders, but team chemistry is still important to productivity. Try as you might, sometimes you have staff members who don't get along and won't work together effectively. I see this on a too-regular basis among the small businesses I coach.

Tensions between two individuals or two departments can have far-reaching effects, taking a toll on your business, slowing production, and making your office feel like a war zone.

Tim, the owner of a heating and cooling company, battles this tension among his small team. His main technician and an assistant must visit client sites and work on the repair jobs together. When they don't get along, the job takes longer or won't be performed to Tim's (or the client's) satisfaction. Ultimately, that hurts sales and revenue.

I've even seen projects sabotaged by other employees to satisfy personal agendas. But who *always* loses? The business owner and the customer.

Minimalists

Comedian George Carlin had this observation about the workforce: "Most people work just hard enough not to get fired and get paid just enough money not to quit."

According to the polling giant, Gallup, Inc., it's true. Gallup's 2010–2012 study, The State of the American Workplace, determined that 70% of U.S. workers are either not engaged in their work or are actively disengaged, with the latter "roaming halls, spreading discontent." Gallup surveyed more than 150,000 full- and part-time workers and concluded that only 30% are engaged and inspired at work. The majority of employees are doing the minimum to get by versus what they're really capable of contributing.[4]

Shrinking margins

How else does employee apathy hurt your enterprise? Through out right theft. Employees who don't have buy-in are more likely to steal, whether it's tangible goods, like office supplies, or "stealing" time in a service environment.

---

[4] http://www.gallup.com/strategicconsulting/163007/state-american-workplace.aspx

The National Federation of Independent Businesses paints a dire picture of the threat to businesses:

> Security experts say that as many as 30% of the average company's employees do steal, and another 60% will steal if given a motive and opportunity. Some estimates indicate that more than $600 billion is stolen annually, or roughly $4,500 per employee. According to the U.S. Department of Commerce, about a third of all business failures each year trace back to employee theft and other employee crime.[5]

Theft of time is less detectable, but just as damaging to your business. Time theft estimates vary from four to five hours a week for the average employee to a frightening 60% to 80% of work time.

A Kansas State University study reported in the scholarly journal, *Computers in Human Behavior,* describes "cyberloafing," or spending time on the computer conducting non-work-related activities. Researchers report that workers spend about 60% to 80% of their time at work surfing non-work-related websites.[6]

Boss burnout

Anyone who has ever launched a business knows that stress goes with the territory; long hours, insufficient family time, and endless decision-making create a pressure-cooker environment, even for those with nerves of steel. Unchecked, the strain can easily lead to burnout, not to mention business failure.

A poor or dysfunctional team can ratchet up the burnout symptoms.

---

[5] http://www. nfib.com/business-resources/business-resources-item?cmsid=29624
[6] http://www.academia.edu/1907790/Conceptualizing_personal_web_usage_in_work_contexts_A_preliminary_framework._Computers_in_Human_Behavior

More of the burden of decision-making and problem solving falls to you, and it's made more difficult by staff squabbles.

Lack of leadership stunts growth

About three-quarters of all U.S. business firms have no payroll. Of the small portion of firms with payroll, the vast majority has only one to four employees. Why do so many businesses get stuck at this level? It's simple. Without additional staff to carry bigger and bigger workloads, your business growth is constrained.

Too many small business owners have trouble delegating, setting the vision, and developing employees. But you can't grow your business if you can't grow your team.

Your growth "set point"

Medicine has the concept of a set point, a particular narrow range at which the body tries to keep at a particular value. Body weight, body temperature, and other functions tend to stick to set points.

I've observed that some business owners have a set point for staff size, revenue size, or market share. Even when spectacular things happen in their businesses that should result in significant growth, within a short period of time something else happens to negate it. A huge contract that doubles your business isn't renewed. Or your fantastic new operations manager leaves for a better situation after only a year.

Having 20 employees requires more time, systems, and development than having five. Expanding staff beyond the numbers you're comfortable with requires consistent team building to deal with chaos and continuously "upgrade" your own leadership skills and those of your team.

When owners ignore team issues, they may unconsciously undermine the growth and lose staff to get back to the comfortable set point.

Can't get no satisfaction

It isn't only the owner who suffers when the team isn't functioning effectively. Employees are unhappy and frustrated, too. Excessive workloads, poor communication, lack of recognition, concerns about leadership's ability to lead the company successfully through challenges – these create a continuous virus of discontent that infects every part of the business.

Without an effective team, quality suffers. Employees have no sense of accountability to the company or the customer, so they hide or push problems down the line for someone else to solve.

Communication breakdowns mean that no one knows what's going on in other departments or, sometimes, even within their own department. There's no macro view of how decisions impact the company as a whole – only the self-serving, territorial lens.

In hostile environments, poor decisions are made because there's no trust. People become afraid of making the wrong decision, thinking, "If I make a mistake, everyone will yell at me."

In some companies, the culture of fear is so strong that employees, attempting to reduce risk as much as possible, actually end up making the wrong decision because it's the one that's viewed as the least risky.

I gotta grow

Without training, development and opportunities to grow, employees get bored with their jobs and leave. As part of its workplace satisfaction survey, the Gallup organization asks employees 12 questions that correlate to employee satisfaction. Several involve learning and developing, including number 12: "This last year, I have had opportunities at work to learn and grow."

What impact does a lack of development have on your business? A big one. According to the 2012 Allied Workforce Mobility Survey, companies lose almost one-quarter of all new employees within a year, and one-third fail to meet productivity targets. The HR professionals responding to the survey cited several factors that limit retention success, such as lack of training and mentoring.

Some employers hesitate to invest in training employees, fearing that the employee will take his newfound knowledge to another organization. That's shortsighted thinking. Training, development, and mentoring actually increase employee retention, which makes these high-return investments. According to the Allied survey, "to fill one position costs on average $10,731, with an additional $21,033 per new hire for relocation."[7]

The employee demand for training and development will increase over the next two decades. Members of the Millennial or Generation Y (roughly, those born between 1982 and 2000) are entering the job market in droves. At twice the size of Generation X, these 75 to 80 million workers and consumers will exert a major influence on the way that businesses operate.

Millennials crave training and development, learning new skills, and feedback. Business owners who don't provide these things will lose the qualities that Millennials can contribute to their organization: continuous learning, team-orientation, collaboration, optimism, achievement, orientation, and knowledge.

---

[7] http://www.alliedhriq.com

Lack of understudies limit growth

Here's another common challenge: no one is being groomed for management, so owners struggle to fill vacant positions. When a person leaves, it's a disaster. Suddenly, you've got a big hole in your operations. Lack of "bench strength" can influence another type of poor managerial behavior: putting up with poor performance. When you have a poor performer on staff, you won't let that person go because you have no one else who can fill the role. Neither of these situations positions a company for growth.

Dancing without a partner

Your team extends to external partners, too. Vendors, strategic alliances, and service providers can help or hinder your business. How do you know when they're hindering? When external "partners" aren't helpful, are too expensive, aren't timely, or don't have enough knowledge.

For example, CPAs are not all created equal. Most are dedicated, forward-thinking advocates for their clients. However, a few are not. They aren't proactive with clients. They don't help their clients understand the big picture.

One of my pet peeves is the CPA who has clients enter all their transactions into QuickBooks. Then, each month, the CPA re-enters the data and creates a monthly financial statement. Not only is this duplicate work wasteful and time-consuming, but the client gets the financial statement three weeks late – too late to act on the data.

One of the biggest sins of external partners is simply waiting to take orders, waiting for you, the owner, to tell them what you need. But if you don't know what you don't know, how is that helping you grow the company?

Why It's Broken

The pressure of being a small business owner is relentless. Increased competition, changing technology, filling multiple roles – *plus* you've got to be a detective, psychoanalyst, leader, coach, and developer of people. For some CEOs, the human resource role doesn't come naturally. Others are oblivious to the ways that they are creating or contributing to the personnel problems within their own organization.

Let's look at some of the most common causes of poorly performing teams.

Hiring process? What process?

Small business owners seldom think of themselves as being in the human resource business. As a result, they don't have consistent hiring processes to follow. Each time there's a position to be filled, it's treated as an isolated incident. Not only does this add stress and chaos to filling a position, it opens the door for hiring mistakes that can cripple your business. Without a consistent process, you may not ask the right questions in the interview or fail to uncover previous employment problems or to convey your expectations of the role.

Focus on the wrong things

Entrepreneurs suffer when they focus on the wrong things in building a great team. If you view paying market-competitive wages or periodic salary increases as an expense "you can't afford" in your business, but you're absorbing high turnover costs because staffers are leaving for a few cents more per hour, your focus must shift. To get the highest return from your employees, you must see them as human capital – as valuable as any other strategy to drive revenue.

Industrialist Henry Ford is lauded by some as a humanitarian for instituting the $5-a-day wage at Ford Motor Company, a substantial increase over the rate paid by competing manufacturers. His move is often attributed to his desire to create his own market, a workforce that could afford to buy the products they were building. However, the real reason that Ford increased the wage so substantially over his competitors was to reduce the turnover that was killing productivity in his factory.

According to a history on the State of Michigan's website, where Ford Motor Company is headquartered:

> Ford's turnover rate was very high. In 1913, Ford hired more than 52,000 men to keep a workforce of only 14,000. New workers required a costly break-in period, making matters worse for the company. Also, some men simply walked away from the line to quit and look for a job elsewhere. Then the line stopped and production of cars halted. The increased cost and delayed production kept Ford from selling his cars at the low price he wanted.[8]

(By the way, the $5 rate wasn't as much a daily wage as a profit-sharing plan that came with a number of strings attached.)

Are you focusing on salary increases you "can't afford" while overlooking the replacement, training, and productivity costs that may be strangling your business?

Pats on the back are free

In the What's Broken section of this chapter, we looked at people issues that challenge owners who've neglected the "team" part of their business. Often it's because the company lacks a system to keep employees engaged and working together effectively. There's no team work, team building, or goal setting. Employees don't understand how their role contributes to achieving the company's vision.

---

[8] http://www. michigan.gov/dnr/0,1607,7-153-54463_18670_18793-53441--,00.html

These owners also lack a system for rewarding good work. (Yep, even recognition and rewards can be systematized.) In fact, many don't even understand that they *need* to reward good work.

Other reasons that bosses overlook performance:

- They're worried that showing appreciation could cause unrecognized employees to feel slighted.

- They feel embarrassed about giving open praise. It's not their style to be effusive.

- The stretched-thin business owner is so caught up in the day-to-day hustle that he doesn't notice that the team needs attention.

- Stoic owners project their own personality traits onto other people: "I don't need a pat on the back. Why should they?"

The bottom line is that the unsuccessful business owners don't understand the correlation between showing appreciation and motivating performance. Instead, they think only about the *cost* of rewards and conclude that it's too expensive.

Are managers born or trained?

Struggling small businesses don't pursue management or leadership training to ensure quality team development. Likewise, they expect employees to learn management skills through osmosis.

I've encountered business after business where a high-performing staffer is promoted to manage a department with no experience or training in managing employees. This leads to a dysfunctional team and a frustrated new manager who secretly wishes he had never been promoted.

Free-range management

While large companies can be guilty of consuming their management team's workweek with unproductive meetings, many small companies make the opposite mistake – they have few, if any meetings. "I don't need to have meetings. We talk all the time," is how these owners justify the lack of formal team gatherings.

This doesn't cut it. It's not easy to track and hold people accountable when you "pop in" and give a task or share an idea. Conversations in passing do not have the same import as a request made in a meeting and documented in a meeting summary.

Dictatorships don't work for long

To get the highest-level performance from your staff, communication between leaders and team members must be reciprocal. That means not just talking, but also *listening.*

Soliciting input from your employees helps your business in two ways:

1. You'll hear valuable business ideas and important issues from those with the most direct experience. As a busy owner, you can become removed from your customer and ways that operations can be improved.

2. Employees with buy-in on decisions will be more likely to "step up," according to a study conducted by John Izzo and reported in *Stepping Up: How Taking Responsibility Changes Everything* (Berrett-Koehler Publishers, 2012):

   > Stepping up means "taking initiative to make the company better, including bringing up new ideas, suggesting better ways of doing business, and taking high levels of effort to improve the organization's services."[9]

Mastering the fine art of accountability

Not having meetings hurts small business owners, but meetings alone won't ensure accountability. That requires finesse on the part of the business owner to properly set expectations, secure commitment, measure progress, and provide feedback.

Too often, owners struggle because they can't find the balance between "nice boss" and "taskmaster," confusing the staff with inconsistency. They operate in opposite extremes: as pushovers wanting to be liked or tyrants demanding unreasonable results.

"Figure it out" is not a training program

What else contributes to team issues in an organization? Not having effective training programs for employees. Submitting them to "trial by fire."

When my friend, Lori, started her new job as the marketing manager of a small environmental software company, her two-week orientation and training program consisted of sitting at her predecessor's desk and reading through files and manuals. After that, she was expected to develop the company's marketing strategy and budget without training on the operations or products of the business.

Why do so many companies, small and large, skimp on this vital development tool? Often, they fear investing in an employee only to have that person leave for the competition. Formal training costs money. Coaching staff takes time. But this creates a vicious cycle: companies don't train workers because they believe they'll just leave, and workers leave because they don't get training.

---

[9] http://www.businessnewsdaily.com/1934-leadership-listening-employee-input-initiative.html

Using the excuse, "I don't have time or the know-how to create a training program" is risky business.

The high costs of bad hires

Without a hiring system, business owners struggle to find and identify good hires. The result? Job vacancies go on longer than they should, or the wrong person is hired just to fill a gap and both scenarios are expensive.

The U.S. Department of Labor currently estimates that the average cost of a bad hiring decision can equal 30% of the individual's first-year potential earnings.[10] That means a single bad hire with an annual income of $30,000 can equal a potential $10,000 loss for the employer. This loss is compounded by the impact of a bad hire on productivity and team morale. One employee with poor skills and attitude can throw an entire department into disorder.

Not just for corporate giants

Here are more negatives that hinder small businesses in building a great team:

- **No formal job duties.** Employees are left to work out among themselves who should be doing what.

- **No written policies.** When employees don't know the rules of the game, they don't feel as though they have a chance to win. Written policies are important so your employees know what's expected of them and so you can hold them to expected standards.

- **No defined culture.** Your company's culture is shorthand for "how we do things around here." It helps you know who to hire, how you manage, and the work values

---

[10] http://www.bbc.com/capital/story/20130719-avoid-costly-hiring-blunders

you expect the team to exhibit. If you can't express your company's culture, you won't know which candidates to select and why, given equal talents, certain employees are just more successful than others in your organization.

A microbusiness owner may eschew policy manuals and culture statements as something for "the big guys." But the successful owners we interviewed realized that from the first employee, a company needs definition and structure to succeed and grow.

Not enough play from your partners

The best service providers act as strategic partners to your business. But too few small business owners create this caliber relationship. They don't demand attention, aren't willing to pay for quality, don't take time to develop relationships, don't have multiple sources so are held hostage, and they don't ask for help. In some instances, the business owner herself is at fault. When you select vendors like a commodity buyer looking for the lowest price, you can't expect to get trusted-advisor-level services.

When you do select service providers who can be partners and long-term advisors for your business, it's vital to treat them with respect. Recently, a friend told me about an incident in her company. Vendors from California flew to Michigan to meet with her and her boss, the company owner. But when they arrived, her boss wasn't there. He'd decided to make a delivery and wouldn't return to the office all that day.

I wondered if the business owner realized the impact of treating vendors poorly on his *own team*. Not only does it damage the business relationship, it sends the message to your employees that you don't respect people or their time.

What Will Fix It

The caliber of your team members can have a tremendous impact on your business. Steve Jobs created a unique culture and one of the most successful companies in the world at Apple. He noticed, "…the dynamic range between what an average person could accomplish and what the best person could accomplish was 50 or 100 to 1. Given that, you're well advised to go after the cream of the cream…. A small team of A+ players can run circles around a giant team of B and C players."[11]

When the economic downturn began, Mike, the owner of an eight-person heating and cooling business, recognized that his team needed a "people upgrade" to boost competitiveness. To improve customer service and accounts receivable, he hired a new inside-office person to respond to customers. Mike saw an immediate return on investment in customer retention and higher accounts receivable turnover.

Culture cures

The successful company leaders I interviewed shared a common characteristic: they could clearly articulate their company's culture. While every organization has a culture, whether you've created it on purpose or allowed it to form organically, not every leader can describe his company's culture.

How do *you* define your company culture? Start by asking yourself questions about the rituals and customs that exist in your company today and those that you *wish* existed.

Still confused about what makes a culture? Try this quick exercise:

- Imagine what would it look like, feel like, and sound like to work as a trader on Wall Street. What kind of customs would they practice?

---

[11] http://www.businessweek.com/smallbiz/news/coladvice/book/bk981106.htm

- Contrast that with what it would look like, feel like, and sound like to work at an Internet startup company in California. What would their rituals and customs be?

- Now imagine picking up the stock trader and the start-up entrepreneur and swapping their locations. Do you think either one would be comfortable or productive in their new work environment? They might eventually adapt, but if they were comfortable where they were originally, chances are they would fail miserably in their new culture.

Do it on purpose

What this means is that you can't create culture by default. You have to purposefully decide what it's going to look like, feel like, and sound like to work at your company, and then strive to make your ideal a reality. That means using two filters:

1. Determine if everyone on your current team is a good fit for the culture you want for your organization.

2. Evaluate all new hires against your company culture. Even a highly qualified candidate may not fit.

Write it down

Want to get clear on your company culture? Put it in writing. (Don't worry about making it perfect. You can always modify and refine your description.)

Start by writing your core values. This can be done either by the owner alone, or by engaging some team members that you believe embody the core values that you want to encourage. Then, to describe your culture, select words that are part of your core values – for instance, "integrity, fun and compassion." Once you've identified the words, write a definition of each word as it applies to your company.

Zingerman's is an Ann Arbor, Michigan-based delicatessen known around the world. In the 30 years since its founding, the company has expanded to include a creamery, restaurants, and a training division, among other businesses. How did a Jewish-style deli in a small Midwestern city become a phenomenon? Zingerman's co-founders credit the strong company culture.

These are Zingerman's guiding principles, the values that form its unique culture:

- Great food
- Great service
- A great place to shop and eat
- Solid profits
- A great place to work
- Strong relationships
- A place to learn
- An active part of our community

Scott, the CEO of an IT services firm I interviewed, shared that involving and empowering the leadership team to create core values and the company's business plan was one of the key factors for recession-proofing his business.

Culture is key for Jim, partner in an automotive manufacturing operation and another study participant. "We have a fun work environment," he said. "It's relaxed with a family atmosphere. For example, we provide lunch every Wednesday to all employees. We have bi-weekly management review meetings and weekly engineering meetings. At least once per week, I walk around the plant and speak with team members as a way to stay connected."

A note of caution when you're shifting a culture: you can't change culture overnight, so you'll have to engage your team to identify ways to roll out and consistently encourage the new culture.

Hire the right people

People are at the heart of company culture. The challenge for growth stems back to whether a company has hired people who share the same vision and have the technical skills to take the company to the next level. If not, growth will be slow. Or non-existent.

Having a strong company culture is an asset for Jason, the founder of the language learning software company. The team is extremely focused because they followed their passion and aligned it with products they believe can be the best in the world. To reinforce that philosophy with new hires, Jason's management team uses an extremely rigorous process to make sure candidates are highly skilled, will love their work, and will fit the culture. "Having figured out how to hire, motivate, and change staff based on alignment with the DNA of who we are has helped us to have a really good team."

On the flip side of hiring the right people is quickly shedding the wrong people. I mentioned that holding onto poor performers too long is one of the biggest team-related mistakes business owners make. This hurts performance, productivity, and morale. Dr. Laith, the leader of a high-growth orthopedic center, offers pragmatic advice, "Don't waste time on employees who aren't working out."

Have a systematic and proven hiring system

Does your business have a systematic hiring process that consistently delivers high-quality candidates? If filling vacant positions is painful and chaotic, try these tips from our top-performing companies:

- Write a list of requirements for each position. List the behavioral attributes needed for the job to be done well.

- Write the help wanted ad from a sales approach. You want to attract the right employees first with language that will make them excited to work for your company and that lets them know whether or not they will fit with your culture. Then, give them the details of the job.

- Know where to find the right candidates. What are the popular information sources for those looking to find careers in your industry? To find out, play the role of the candidate and perform a broad Internet search to see what help wanted ad sites appear in the search results.

- List all sourcing options other than paid advertising, such as referrals from employees, vendors, and job fairs. Keep on top of sourcing trends because they change on a regular basis. Also, consider having a page on your website to capture information from interested candidates on a regular basis.

- Determine an advertising and/or referral rewards budget based on the importance of finding the right candidates.

- Write interview questions in advance. This is no time to wing it! Employment laws can be tricky, and you want to make sure you conduct interviews fairly and are comparing "apples to apples."

- When it's interview time, use behavior-based questions. These are designed to show how a person thinks and acts based on previous situations, such as:
    - What's an example of how you've worked on a team?
    - Have you handled a difficult situation? How did you handle it?
    - What do you do if you disagree with someone at work?

        ❑ How were you able to motivate employees or co-workers?

If you can afford it, pay a consultant for assessments. As I mentioned in the chapter on sales, assessments are designed to help employers make good hiring decisions by measuring how well a person will perform a job. Assessments can identify a candidate's true strengths and challenges much better than simply interviewing, but they can be expensive. Savvy owners typically decide whether to use assessments based on the importance of the job.

Specialty construction company founder, Tom, shares his simple (but not easy) recipe for building a successful team: hire a motivated person, teach and train that person, then coach and hold them accountable. "We hire employees that are over-achievers," says Tom. "They think the same way in terms of our company values. We've also grown our own talent internally by looking for interns who were technologically talented and then leveraged that."

Orienting for success

Once you've hired your new superstars, have a plan to bring them into the organization in a methodical way. Sitting in the corner reading a manual for two weeks is not an orientation plan!

"Onboarding" is a fancy human resources term. Stripping away the corporate jargon, it means that you have a plan and process to introduce new employees to your company – its products and services, its systems, and its culture. It's a systematic introduction to everything an employee needs to know to be a star contributor at your company. Not sure how to get started orienting new team members? Mentally "walk through" a day or week in your new employee's role. What does he need to know? Where can he find help? Brainstorm a list of policies, procedures, introductions and tours, position information, and information systems (computer programs, passwords, Internet, and email.) Use this to create a checklist for all new hires.

If it's important, document it

Not everything team-related in your small business has to be documented, but here are some areas that our successful owners found helpful:

- **Policies manual or employee handbook.** Experts say that small and mid-sized businesses can craft employee manuals that both protect them from litigation and put staff members at ease by spelling out the company's policies in positive terms. They should be based on what's important to the company, but generally outline what's expected of the employee as well as what the employee can expect. They typically include pay and compensation decisions, performance review procedures, benefits, flex-time, and complaint or dispute resolution procedures.

   Having an accurate up-to-date employee handbook or policies manual can protect your company from some legal actions, but the law is complex and ever-changing, so you should always consult an attorney to ensure that it's been written properly.

   An article on *Inc.* magazine's website, Inc.com, titled "What to include in an employee handbook," is a great resource for business owners.

- **Process manuals.** Process manuals outline how to do a job. They are typically used for routine tasks and/or where it is important to be consistent. For example, fast-food restaurants created systems to serve their food in record time. That process or system is written down in manuals and illustrated in diagrams as employee guides.

The simpler and more straightforward the process, the better.

To easily create a process, follow the approach I described at the end of Chapter 4, Get Efficient and Stay That Way. Start by writing each step on a sticky note. Next, place each sticky note on a wall in the order they should flow. Allow those involved with the process to review the steps and move, combine, or eliminate steps, if needed to improve the flow. Then, write down the process.

Another approach is to have new employees write down each step as you teach a process. That will help them remember the process and start the documentation!

Of course, once you create it, you need to review processes regularly (at least annually) to ensure work is being done as efficiently as possible. The good news is that it was once a logistical nightmare for businesses to keep process manuals up to date. But with "shared drives," electronic manuals can now be updated centrally, and employees can access the updated materials at any time, rather than having to print them.

Return on engagement

Hiring the right people and documenting your processes are concrete steps to building a great team. Having your employees engaged in the work they're doing is just as important to business growth, but not as simple as checking off a list.

Don't let that deter you! Remember Gallup's poll showing that 70% of workers are not engaged in their work. It's important for the health of your business that your employees are in the 30% column.

So what do you have to do to engage employees? Here are a few ideas:

- **Provide the time and opportunity for your team to get to know each other as** *people.* Company outings, a pleasant place to eat lunch, time to chat with a friend – those are all important elements to helping your employees feel a human connection to the company and each other.

- **Give them the chance to be heard and appreciated.** Employees don't typically leave companies because of pay; they leave because they aren't appreciated or listened to.

- **Talk to them about their career path.** Even small businesses can dream big. One way to demonstrate opportunity within your company is to create and share an organization chart showing what the company will look like in the long term. If your employees see a fit, you can talk about the part you'll both play to reach that vision.

- **Don't forget personal growth.** Are you and your employees honing your personal skills like listening, self-confidence, a sense of humor, and empathy? As human beings, we all seek to improve these skills. Including areas that a team member wants to improve as part of their professional growth can be crucial to engagement.

- **Give them an opportunity to support the community.** This can be done as a group such as volunteering at a food bank or home build site, or on an individual basis by allowing employees to volunteer during work hours, or matching contributions to their favorite charity.

Each of these ideas will help engage your team and, as those owners we interviewed can attest, it can make a material difference to your bottom line.

Need more proof? According to an article by Christopher Seward in the *Atlanta Journal-Constitution*, "Gallup Chairman and CEO Jim Clifton noted that the most engaged workers 'come up with most of the innovative ideas, create most of a company's new customers, and have the most entrepreneurial energy.' And there are other benefits: They also have nearly 50% fewer accidents, 41% fewer quality defects, and far less healthcare costs, researchers said."[12]

Development and coaching

Hiring star candidates creates a strong foundation for your team. To capitalize on your team's potential, you'll need to add continuous development and coaching.

Chapter 1 of the Success Code focused on planning in depth, but the team also needs to create their own goals and plans, and then understand how their goals support the big picture. They can't pull together if they don't know where they're going.

Personal development plans are a powerful way to link employees' personal and professional development with the growth of your business. The best development plans include training, stretch assignments, rotation (experiencing other departments and roles), and self-reflection.

Does it cost money and time to develop and coach employees? You bet. Does the employer receive a return on investment? A big *yes!*

A note of caution: be aware of how you spend your leadership time. It's easy to invest 80% of your time on the bottom 20% of performers in your organization. It's easy to believe that "fixing what's not working"

---

[12] http://www. ajc.com/weblogs/biz-beat/2013/jun/24/gallup-blame-managers-dis-engaged-workers/

will yield the biggest return on investment, but that's actually false. Developing your top performers even further will increase their effectiveness beyond any incremental gains from the poor performers.

For more on this concept, read *First, Break all the Rules, What the World's Greatest Managers Do Differently by Marcus Buckingham and Curt Coffman* (Simon and Schuster, 1999).

Recognition and rewards

People crave positive feedback. They relish recognition of their efforts – acknowledgment of peers and leaders, the glow that comes with knowing an achievement has been noticed and celebrated. To properly recognize and reward your team, it's important to understand what motivates each individual (ask them!) and to use that information to reinforce excellent performance.

Sherman, owner of a waste management company, believes that keeping his employees involved and motivated in continuously improving company operations and customer service pays off. He uses a performance-based pay system for most of the staff. Employee of the month, NASCAR tickets, cash bonuses for hard work and spontaneous pats

on the back round out his motivation strategies. It's working: employee turnover is 15% lower than the industry average, saving him tens of thousands of dollars each year.

Put your partners to work

Just like your internal team, you must select your external team – your service providers and vendors – with care, building a strong business partnership.

Here are the simple (but again, not easy) steps to successful partnering that I uncovered during my study:

1. Have a process for vetting new vendors. Use your culture as a filter to select those who are match for your philosophy and approach.

2. Be proactive about what you want from them. Don't make them guess about your performance expectations.

3. Create a relationship with them. Remember, it's a two-way street.

One of my business practices I recommend to all of my clients is this: each year, organize a meeting where you bring in your most important external "partners." Often, it includes your CPA, business coach, attorney, and financial planner, although you may include others. Bring them to your office for a one-hour meeting and *pay them for their time.*

Here's your loose agenda:

- Strategize for the next year.

- Ask what these pros advise, based on their knowledge of their subject matters and trends.

- Discuss how you can improve in your business.

- Looking at cash flow, long-term financial structuring, legal protections, determine what you should be striving for and looking out for.

- Create a long-term plan.

When you conduct this annual strategic planning session with your most important service providers, it can create a secondary benefit. My clients who've done this say that it spurs their advisors to compete with each other to offer the best advice or solutions.

CHAPTER SUMMARY
Build an Exceptional Team

Key Points

Success Code, Principle #7: Successful business owners know that to sustain momentum and forward motion, they must create an employee-centered culture.

- You must sincerely care about your team if you want to be an effective leader.

- Employers must be clear on their own vision for the company so they can convey it to their team.

- Take time to define your business's culture and be sure everyone knows what is expected.

- Hiring only when your business gets busy is not an intelligent way to grow your company.

- Spend more time developing A+ workers than improving C or D workers.

- As an owner, delegate work so you don't burn out yourself. Without an effective team, starting at the top, quality suffers.

- Without training, the best workers often quit.

- Have a succession plan for every position and every external partner.

- As a leader, you are automatically in the human resource business.

- Reward people as they want to be rewarded.

- Continually ask for input from your employees so they feel a sense of ownership.

- Plan how you will interview, orient, and train new employees.

- Create policy and position manuals.

- Hold a yearly meeting with your external partners to establish your path forward.

CHAPTER 8
Give, Then Give Some More

When economies falter, it seems like everyone is looking for a deal. As a business owner, you can fall into the habit of discounting as a strategy, but the successful owners we interviewed knew that, long-term, a practice like that can prove costly and ruin profitability. So "give" in this chapter title doesn't mean giving away profits. Instead, owners who truly understand "survival skills" know how to hold onto customers with increased service levels, how to provide outstanding product and service offerings, and how to stay in front of the emerging needs of potential new customers. Successful owners understand that by giving more now, they ensure the long-term success of the company.

As you go about your day today, tune into your experiences with businesses. From coffee houses, grocery stores, and restaurants to customer service lines and community resources, you are served by dozens of organizations every day. How often is your experience remarkable? And how often is it poor or downright frustrating?

Studies show that business owners can't accurately judge the level of customer service their companies provide. Global consulting firm Bain & Company reports, "90% of companies say they provide excellent customer service, yet only 8% of customers say the same."[1] That's some disconnect!

When the recession took hold, the small business leaders I interviewed acted swiftly to reduce costs, improve efficiency, and expand market share with some reduced prices. But common among the most successful owners was the understanding that they couldn't price their way out of the recession. These smart CEOs knew that doubling down

---

[1] http://www.bain.com/bainweb/pdfs/cms/hottopics/closingdeliverygap.pdf

on value through extraordinary service and quality was the key to outlasting any economic challenge.

Big cost of poor service

Companies have forgotten how to serve the customer to create remarkable service, and it's costing them. A lot. Consider this stat highlighted by the Center for Media Research:

> Genesys, with research firm Greenfield Online and Datamonitor/Ovum analysts, measuring the cost of poor customer service in the U.S., found that enterprises in the U.S. lose an estimated $83 billion each year due to defections and abandoned purchases as a direct result of a poor experience.[2]

That's $83 billion – with a "B" – and it includes business lost to competitors and business lost to the industry.

It doesn't have to be that way.

Stand out with customer service

The leaders I interviewed know that customer service *is* a business differentiator; *66% of consumers are willing to spend more* with a company they believe provides excellent customer service.[3]

An example of a company providing remarkable customer service is Zappos.com. (In fact, calling out Zappos' customer service has become a cliché in business literature. And yet, rival service-leading companies seem to be few and far between.) But why do business experts continue to highlight Zappos.com as a compelling customer service story?

---

[2] http://www.mediapost.com/publications/article/122502/
[3] http://www.businessweek.com/magazine/content/10_23/b4181088591033.htm

To put it bluntly, they built a company from startup to $1 billion in sales in just 10 years. Zappos.com began as an online shoe retailer that baked customer service into its business model. CEO Tony Hsieh said in a Bloomberg Business interview in 2005, "I wanted us to have a whole company built around [customer service]."[4]

Another interview with Hsieh in *Tech Republic* illustrates the impact of remarkable customer service. "The primary sources of the company's rapid growth have been repeat customers and numerous word-of-mouth recommendations. Of its customers, 75% are repeat buyers."[5]

Remarkable service: so rare that people talk about it

This company's customer service reputation has spread virally as well: "When Zappos offered special return shipping assistance beyond their company policies...the good word about the company spread quickly throughout the blogosphere."[6]

Fifty to 100 years ago, businesses thrived *despite* poor service. Your local bank staff might have been elitist, saving all their smiles for customers with the biggest deposits, but because it was the only game in town, you suffered brusque treatment. Today, you can bank anywhere, anytime.

During the last century, mammoth businesses selling low-priced consumer goods, like Gillette, simply flooded the market with advertising, knowing that every dollar spent on advertising its razors brought three in revenue. Not so, post-millennium. Today's buyers are more likely to buy based on service rather than brand. In fact, a study

---

[4] http://www.businessweek.com/magazine/content/10_23/b4181088591033.htm
[5] Cerny, Jeff. 10 questions on customer service and "delivering happiness": an interview with Tony Hsieh Tech Republic. October 1, 2009.
[6] Exceptional Service, Exceptional Profit: The Secrets of Building a Five-Star Customer Service Organization, Leonardo Inghilleri and Micah Solomon, Amacom Books (New York), p. 116, 2010

by Dimensional Research shows that customer service is *the most important factor* influencing buying decisions.[7]

No doubt, delivering outstanding service is easier to talk about than to execute. Global competition, together with social networks, online review sites, and instant communication tools, has raised service level expectations. Unhappy customers can broadcast their negative opinions and experiences to the world. But companies can reap huge rewards when they wow customers with great service.

Let's take a closer look at what happens when a business suffers from customer service scarcity.

What's Broken

The impact of poor customer service is felt far beyond the isolated transaction. Poor service and inferior products cost companies revenue, affect reputation, squeeze profits, and limit growth. It can even kill companies.

Word of mouth: boon or bane?

Word of fantastic customer service spreads. Unfortunately, word of dismal customer service goes spreads, too. Only farther and faster.

Of customers who've had a good experience, 87% will tell others. One-third will tell five or more people. But even more people (95%) who've had a *bad* experience will tell others. And more than half of those (54%) will tell five or more people.[8]

A few years ago, I coached a company with serious service issues. They were making mistakes with their customers. Orders were wrong or

---

[7] http://cdn.zendesk.com/resources/whitepapers/Zendesk_WP_Customer_Service_and_Business_Results.pdf

[8] http://www.bain.com/bainweb/pdfs/cms/hottopics/closingdeliverygap.pdf

late. Clients complained. Even when the company fixed the incorrect orders, the negative effects lived on. Word of mouth spread. The vicious cycle continued because the company's process itself was broken. They would fix the mistakes after they were made, but they never solved the root cause of the problems. Customers lost confidence in the organization.

My experience *is* your reputation

Here's a recent lesson in the power of customer experience to make – or break – reputations. Having been a business coach and advisor for eight years now, my company has grown, along with the complexity of my marketing, sales, and operations. I wanted someone knowledgeable about websites, customer relationship management software, and marketing automation tools to look at where my business is today and where it's going, and advise me on the technology I'd need to make it all work as seamlessly as possible.

I did some research, then reached out to two different "systems experts" for a consultation, using contact forms on their websites.

No response. I sent an email to each. Still no response. It's now been over two months and, after not hearing from providers who were supposed to be experts in business systems, it's too late. The fact that both systems failed destroyed their credibility as "systems experts."

I'm not alone in my reaction; 91% of customers say they won't go back to a company after just *one* bad customer service experience.[9]

What's more, my experience proves a scary fact – businesses can be undermined by customer service and systems failures in their organizations and *not even know it.*

---

[9] http://www.bain.com/bainweb/pdfs/cms/hottopics/closingdeliverygap.pdf

Trial, but no repeat business

The proliferation of new businesses and the ease of buying online have given consumers more options to explore.

Service was "meh"? Products just okay but not great? It's almost effortless to let your fingers do the searching for another provider.

Increased competition and ease of finding alternatives make it harder to hold on to customers. And that makes a big impact on the bottom line: repeat customers spend more money and generate higher profits.

According to a new analysis by SumAll, a New York-based analytics company that tracks commerce data for more than 30,000 companies, 25% to 40% of the total revenues of the most stable businesses in the SumAll network come from repeat business. In fact, businesses with a 40% level of repeat customers generated 47% more revenue than similar businesses that only had 10% of their customers returning.[10]

Repeat customers are key to higher profits

High customer churn is costly, in dollars, time, and energy. You've heard the statistic that it's five to seven times more expensive to get a new customer than to retain a current customer. And we saw from the SumAll analysis that companies with a higher percentage of repeat customers are more profitable.

Let's break down the reasons why having more repeat customers equals higher profits:

1. **Repeat customers spend more on each purchase than new customers.** Dane Atkinson, Chief Executive of

---

[10] http://www.smallbusiness.foxbusiness.com/marketing-sales/2013/04/26/how-to-get-customers-to-come-back/

SumAll, reports, "Across our 30,000 sellers, returning customers spend 2.6 times that of one-time buyers."

2. **Repeat customers are more profitable than new customers.** The margins are higher on these purchases as well, because the business has no added costs associated with acquiring the customer.

Industries have average costs of customer acquisition. If your business has a higher percentage of repeat customers than your competitors, then you likely have a lower average customer acquisition cost, and that equals a competitive advantage. The effect can be even more pronounced in retail and restaurant industries, where acquisition costs are high and costs to serve customers are relatively low.

If the reverse is true – if you have a lower-than-average percentage of repeat customers than your competitors – then your customer acquisition cost is higher, your profits are lower and company growth will lag other companies in your industry. Competitive *dis*advantage.

Ideal customers are lost

I recently saw a joke motivational poster. You know the ones that feature a photo of a beautiful mountain and an inspiring phrase? This one had the word "Apathy" in bold letters, followed by this line: "If we don't take care of the customer, maybe they'll stop bugging us."

For business owners, it's a vicious cycle. Apathy among your employees contributes to poor customer service, and the impacts of poor customer service generate apathy among staff.

Employee exodus

It's no coincidence that companies with poor service and products have low levels of employee engagement. Employees want to feel that they are part of something bigger than themselves, that they have an important mission. Promoting and providing poor-quality products or services doesn't engender pride. It's demoralizing to work for a company that you can't be proud of.

It can be hard for an organization to break out of this cycle. When good employees are hired, they soon leave, so the company is continuously hiring and training, never able to gain traction.

I learned this lesson early in my career. One of my early jobs after college was working for a telecommunications company as a salesperson. This was during a time period when telecommunications was less stable than it is now. In fact, we used to call it the "wild, wild West" because so many companies started and the owners made big bucks. As inexperienced business owners, they also overpaid salespeople who, in turn, promised customers the world to make sales quotas.

During my first day on the job, I dutifully called current customers to set up appointments for potential add-on sales. The first five people I spoke with each told me that if I had any integrity I'd quit soon because of my employer's pitiful service and lack of honesty. Their predictions came true – I quit within a few days.

Firefighting leads to burnout

Fixing customer screw-ups saps your time and energy as an entrepreneur. If you and your team spend all your resources scrambling to get new customers to replace those lost, you can't upgrade products or services in your organization.

Your products grow stagnant. Other companies (those with higher customer retention rates and lower acquisition costs) make continuous improvements in their products and services, gaining new customers each week. The margin between your company and your competitors' profits grows ever wider.

Consistency matters

Without clear customer service standards and training in place, service and product quality is inconsistent from one customer to the next. When customers don't know what to expect, they are skeptical, unsure, and reluctant to buy.

Variations on customer experience can occur within your company, too. Will your training department treat the customer like royalty, going the extra mile and giving an incredible experience, while the service department ignores the customer and dodges the responsibility for any problems?

Substandard product offerings and poor customer service have a greater impact on your business than many other more attention-grabbing business topics. Innovation or cutting-edge technology means little to the client who can't use your service because of delivery snafus.

Why It's Broken

No one sets out to provide poor service. It doesn't appear in any company's mission statement. Yet it happens. Well-intentioned business owners find themselves undermined by high customer churn, high employee turnover, and high acquisition costs.

Let's zero in on a few of the most common causes of customer service breakdowns.

Culture clash

In some businesses, quality isn't a core value, so poor performance is tolerated. Company leaders believe that other characteristics will overcome any service failings.

A few years ago, I crossed paths with an engineering firm whose leaders believed that their employees' personal relationships with decision makers in client organizations would overcome any and all quality issues. To increase profit margins, the firm used inexperienced engineers to draw plans for projects. And if those novice engineers caused costly problems because of mistakes on plans, well, they relied on the drinking-buddy relationships to forgive the errors. This relationship-trumps-all approach worked back when the founders ran the company 50 years ago, but it doesn't now.

I'm giving good service, right?

Even small businesses that *do* value quality can suffer when service and product standards have not been defined. Your staff simply may not know *how* to give consistent, high-quality service or to create consistent, high-quality products.

I see this happen often in businesses once they've grown past the startup stage. In the early days of the company, the owner controls a lot. It's his baby, so the standards are high. As the company grows, the owner *assumes* that everyone knows and cares like he does, so he doesn't create written standards and procedures.

Unfortunately, the growth point is also the customer service failure point. The employees aren't malicious. They just don't have the same depth of experience or desire as the founder to give a high-quality experience.

Just let me do my work

Owners who prefer to spend their time on the technical side of their business often neglect general management functions. They fail to clearly communicate expectations, to document, or to hold staff members accountable. Businesses like these have no mechanism or appetite to really listen to customers. The organizational attention is focused on practicing a skill rather than creating the right systems to support quality.

Owners who spend their days deep in projects can't guess what customers actually want or how they rate your products and services. You must have ways to solicit and capture that feedback. And perhaps hardest of all, you have to *act* on that information.

The founder's ego can get in the way of soliciting honest feedback from customers. When your business is your baby, you don't want to hear about problems in your products or services. An outgrowth of this characteristic is that employees don't bring problems to you because they know it'll raise your ire.

Silence is deadly

Systems breakdowns like the ones I mentioned earlier in the chapter leave customers frustrated when they report a problem and are met with silence from the organization. It's not actually having a problem that makes customers angry; it's not hearing a response.

In an article on Entrepreneur.com about customer service, software company founder Ross Kimbarovsky writes, "After answering hundreds of thousands of customer support requests, we've discovered that a big source of customer service frustration is silence, not the actual time it takes to answer a customer's question or resolve their problem."[11]

No power to your people

Businesses with poor products and services often haven't empowered employees to be part of the solution. When a staffer brings a problem to the boss and is told to "handle it" but isn't given the authority to resolve the issue, the employee learns to pass the blame.

A friend told me her story of working for a large national bank. The corporation spent tens of thousands of dollars on a campaign touting a reputation for stellar service. Employees were urged to do everything within their power to satisfy the customer – except to waive any fees.

Because the vast majority of customer complaints were related to fees – unintended overdrafts, fees for cashing checks, minimum balance fees, and the like – employees saw the "empowerment" campaign as empty and even hypocritical. That meant tens of thousands of dollars were wasted.

Employees at Zappos.com have the opposite attitude because the company has turned the entire call center system on its head. Typical call centers have a regimented process. Call center representatives have no authority to resolve customer complaints, are allowed only to follow a script, and are evaluated based on the brevity of the call. Is it surprising that call centers have the highest employee turnover rates – 26% to 33% – of any industry?[12]

Here's how Zappos does it differently. The online retailer's customer service agents, who undergo *seven weeks of training* on how to make customers happy before they're set loose in the call center, are taught to be fanatical about pleasing customers. The 500+ call center staffers are evaluated on customer satisfaction, not the length of the call. In fact, Zappos spokeswoman Diane Coffey shared that in December 2012, a "client loyalty agent" recorded the company's longest call to date: 10 hours and 29 minutes.

Now, a 10-hour phone call might sound like a crazy thing for a company to allow. But as Jeffrey Lewis, Customer Loyalty Team

[11] http://www.entrepreneur.com/article/227458#ixzz2iTNhuo37

[12] http://www. smallbusiness.chron.com/standard-employee-turnover-call-center-industry-36185.html

Supervisor, told the *Huffington Post,* "Zappos' first core value is deliver wow through service, and we feel that allowing our team members the ability to stay on the phone with a customer for as long as they need is a crucial means of fulfilling this value."[13]

Lack of training

The seven weeks of training that Zappos' call center staffers get is an industry anomaly. The vast majority of small businesses have little, if any, training for customer service. And ongoing training to continuously upgrade customer service skills? Forget it.

Instead of dismissing training as luxury that's unattainable, small businesses would do better to think creatively about unique ways to get training for staffers. Ask a vendor to sponsor training. Team up with another non-competing company and share the costs of group training. Use web-based training tools.

Quality – a moving target

It's challenging for employees to deliver quality products and services when the company hasn't defined what quality looks like. It's even tougher to measure quality when there are no standards.

Lack of specificity and standards can lead to other measurement shortcomings: managers don't use quality as part of employee success measurement, so employees aren't accountable. I can sympathize.

Determining a rating system for quality or customer satisfaction seems complex, especially drilling down to the individual staff level. So what happens? Managers and owners forgo all efforts to rate and measure quality, and fail to even discuss it with employees.

---

[13] [http://www.huffingtonpost.com/2012/12/21/zappos-10-hour-call_n_2345467.html]

Leaders' egos can preclude focus on customer service or quality. Viewing it as a soft skill, shortsighted business owners feel that they are too busy growing the business to worry about touchy-feely initiatives.

Remember the $83 billion in lost business credited to poor customer service? If your business is a bucket and your bucket has holes, customers and revenue pour out. Shouldn't that get your attention?

An ounce of prevention...

For time-starved business owners, creating processes and training for customer service seems time-consuming when resources are needed elsewhere in the business. Really, it's preventative medicine. The lagging indicators – lost revenues, rework – far outweigh the initial investment in standards and procedures for great customer service.

Case in point: Eric owns a small construction and handyman service. Two years ago, he hit an overwhelmingly busy week. To take on two projects at once, he assigned a pair of new employees to perform a rush job for a customer. Eric was concerned that he'd lose the rush job if he told the customer he'd need extra time to train his new staffers. But at the end of the project, the client wasn't satisfied with the work performed by the newbies, so Eric had to tear out the work and redo it. What was the cost of doing that project twice compared with a little extra time training staff?

Setting a standard that's out of reach

There is no cookie-cutter customer service standard that applies to every business. It depends on your target market. I believe consistency of service is more important than providing the highest level of service. Chains like McDonald's and Five Guys both sell hamburgers, but customers have a different service expectation for each brand. At McDonald's the cost is lower, and expectations are lower, too. A more costly burger joint needs a larger staff, higher-paid employees, and classier accouterments.

Take my own business: I'm a high-end coach. My clients invest not-insignificant sums to work with me, and most of those relationships are long term. When I bring on a new client, I select a high-quality, personalized gift. My business spends a great deal on client appreciation, because high touch is part of my brand. It's the experience that I want my clients to associate with working with me.

Bottom line: Don't offer Cadillac service for a Chevy price *unless* you can offer it consistently.

Not hiring for service skills

In too many small businesses, customer service abilities aren't taken into account when hiring. The interviewers don't ask questions about past customer service experience, fail to assess a candidate's service ethic, and don't emphasize a culture of service with new hires.

If you want your business to have a culture of customer service, it must apply to every employee in the organization, not just those with "customer service representative" as a title.

Equipment fail

Trying to scrimp on equipment purchases or technology upgrades? Make sure that your quality doesn't suffer because of it. Employees who are forced to use outdated systems or equipment that breaks down won't be able to provide service and products that repeat customers expect. One of my pet peeves is working with printing companies that don't have the latest version of graphic design software. This causes my team extra time, phone calls, and expense to resolve compatibility issues between designers and printers.

When you do have the latest technology, make sure that you also invest in training. What good is that powerful customer relationship management system (CRM) if no one knows how to use it?

Not using the tools

Another way that small businesses can lose the customer service game is by failing to keep up with trends or new ways to deliver excellent customer service. Maybe letting customers send you a tweet on Twitter or sending an instant message via an electronic feedback application on your website would let you resolve more issues, more quickly.

Out of touch with reality

When businesses start out, the founder often handles many of the day-to-day operations. After the business expands, it outpaces the owner's ability to handle everything himself. Before he knows it, he's removed from what's happening on the customer level.

By the time the recession hit hard in 2008, many small business owners realized that they had become isolated from customers. During the boom times, they hired people to manage the day-to-day interactions.

Even huge companies with dedicated customer teams can lose the line of sight between customers who buy your products and the leaders who make the decisions. It can take a bold move to repair the damage caused by disconnection.

In 2008, Domino's Pizza's sales fell, and its stock hit a record low. Yet in 2010, when restaurants in general were doing poorly because recession-weary consumers pulled back on spending, Domino's stock had gained 233%, compared with 37% for its closest rival, Papa John's.

What happened in those two years to put Domino's on the upswing?

According to an article in *Bloomberg BusinessWeek*, the Ann Arbor, Michigan, chain spent millions on a "brutally honest" advertising campaign saying that some people thought its pizza "sucked." Domino's then changed its recipe, offered a money-back guarantee, and embraced social media and e-commerce to engage consumers.

CEO J. Patrick Doyle said the rebranding effort addressed the "elephant in the room" – the fact that many customers didn't like the pizza. Domino's campaign condemning the quality of its own products inspired millions of customers to take another chance on the pizza precisely because it was a bold and unconventional move.[14]

Admitting your company's failings takes guts. Not every business owner has the fortitude. Reluctance to hear criticism stops most entrepreneurs from asking their customers (and non-buyers) for feedback. As the founder of your company, complaints are akin to a personal attack. It's like someone calling your baby *ugly*.

Only by going to the source – your customers – and listening to the uncomfortable truth can you take action to regain lost loyalty. But the goodwill and increased revenues are worth the momentary damage to your ego.

What Will Fix It

When I interviewed 50 business owners who'd successfully survived the recession and asked them to share their best practices, I expected that most would credit cost-cutting or improving efficiency as the reasons they'd remained profitable while others went out of business.

Yes, there were cost reductions. And more focus on efficiency. But what surprised me was that the most successful small business leaders

---

[14] http://www. businessweek.com/news/2011-10-17/domino-s-brutally-hon-est-ads-offset-slow-consumer-spending.html

believed that the practice *most responsible* for their success was their renewed focus on the customer.

Certain business owners, like Tom, built his specialty construction firm on the foundation of deep customer knowledge. Service is both a core value and a differentiator of his company. He said, "Our customers tell us, 'Your ability to understand what my challenges are and your ability to develop solutions and help me become successful sets you apart from the other companies that do the same thing.'"

Others, like restaurant owner Noe, who created his own *Undercover Boss* scenario when he started delivering food to his patrons to get their honest opinions, sprang into action as the economy sank.

Let's take a closer look at how these leaders outlasted the Great Recession and have continued to prosper with increased service levels and identifying emerging customer needs.

Have a vision, write it down

Great service and products start with a strong foundation: the vision. My study's most successful leaders had a clear vision of what quality products and service look like for their company. They were specific and put it in writing.

I'm a stickler for specificity and documentation. Most of my customers have a culture statement that identifies who they are, how they are going to treat people, and their company's customer service standards. The culture statement becomes shorthand for "how we do things around here."

Not all of them have their quality procedures and standards as specifically diagrammed as I would like. In fact, that's a pitfall for most companies – they just don't get specific enough. Defining clear and repeatable standards of care requires thinking through every detail of the answers to seemingly mundane questions, such as:

> *How are we going to answer the phone?*
> *How are we going to deliver the product?*
> *What are the standards?*

"We return all phone calls within 24 hours" is a customer service standard that's easily understood and measurable. When creating your culture statement, define what behavioral attributes are necessary to ensure high quality and include those words in the statement.

Tom keeps customer satisfaction top of mind with this list of Guiding Principles for Success, posted at every employee's workstation:

- Take care of the customer at *any* cost.

- Under-promise and over-deliver.

- Always make your client look good to their customer.

- Be known as the resource, not the problem to be managed.

- Understand what the customer needs before your competition.

- Never burn bridges.

- Use your instinct and passion to decide "the right thing to do."

- Be a team together and a team apart.

- Our success is a result of great performance and 100% customer satisfaction.

- Remember, we are only as good as our last project!

Know the ROI

Make sure that you understand the return on investment if you improve your products and services. Take it down to dollars and cents.

Staffing levels?
Training?
New technology?
Quality of raw materials that go into the product?

What is our return on investment if we raise our game? Can we charge higher prices? Can we attract a higher caliber of customer? Get more repeat business?

Get creative about customer service

Do your homework and know what's happening in your industry, but also look outside your own industry for ideas about how to improve.

Know what your competition is doing, but don't be handcuffed by them. Innovate to stand out from the pack! Think creatively. You may be able to add features, services, or additional "bonuses" that create a higher perceived value but don't cost your company a lot of time or money.

Here's an example highlighted in an article on Entrepreneur.com. The Airport Fast Park at the Baltimore Washington International Airport is a "park-n-ride" shuttle. But it does a few things that set it apart from other shuttle services. The article stated, "While on the bus, the friendly driver actually talks to you, and on your way back, the shuttle takes you directly to your car, with a complimentary bottle of water."[15]

Every time that I return from a flight, I'm tired and dehydrated. Having a bottle of water waiting for me on the shuttle ride to my car is a low-cost gesture that would have a strong impact on my shuttle experience.

It starts at the top

Understand that a culture of service starts at the top. As the owner, you have to provide outstanding service to your *team* as well as your *customers*. How often do you blow off a meeting with your staff or show up late? How do you talk to them when they come to you with a problem? Do you preach honesty but skirt the boundaries of ethical behavior yourself? If you set the standard for acceptable behavior, your staff will imitate it with your customers.

Earlier in my career, when I reported to the CEO of a company, I referred a friend as a terrific candidate for a high-level position. The CEO spent an hour with my friend, excitedly talking about his vision for the company and all the things the two of them had in common. Post-meeting, the collegiality was gone. The CEO didn't respond to any of my friend's attempts to follow up. I was embarrassed that the CEO treated my friend so poorly and felt that his behavior reflected on me, too. How many people do you think I referred to the company following that incident? That's right, zero.

The team's the thing

The importance of building a customer-centric team was a recurring theme in my conversations with successful small business owners. Interviewee Denise owns a promotional products company doing nearly $1 million in revenue each year. She summed up this point perfectly: "You're no one without your team. Have a good team behind you to give great customer service."

---

[15] http://simplecomplexity.net/stories-of-good-and-bad-customer-service/

I often heard comments like this one from Bob and Cathy, owners of a cleaning and restoration service: "Our guys actually care about doing a good job for the customers, where other companies are only worried about the bottom line. In the long run, that makes us more successful."

I encourage my clients to set SMART goals that identify quality and hold everyone accountable for achieving them. Those might be reducing returns by a certain percentage each quarter or increasing return visits within a specified timeframe. What's important is that the goals are specific, measurable, attainable, realistic, and time-bound – and that the entire team is involved in achieving them.

Train, then train some more

Customer service and quality can't happen through osmosis. They require specific, detailed documentation of quality procedures and customer service standards.

Zappos isn't the only name brand renowned for customer service. There's a reason that Apple Stores boast the highest per-foot revenue of any retailer. Technology website Gizmodo wrote about the contents of Apple's secret Genius (the moniker given to Apple's technical troubleshooters) training manual:

> *We read Apple's secret Genius training manual from cover to cover. It's a penetrating look inside Apple: psychological mastery, banned words, roleplaying – you've never seen anything like it. It reinforces the fact that nothing at the Apple Store is taken for granted. From the way you are greeted when you walk into the store to the way Genius Bar experts communicate with agitated customers, Apple carefully considers the experience its customers have at every touchpoint.*[16]

---

[16] http://www. forbes.com/sites/carminegallo/2012/08/30/apples-secret-employee-training-manual-reinvents-customer-service-in-seven-ways/

That's the key to developing proper customer standards and training: *carefully considering the experience your customers have at every touchpoint.* Put yourself in the position of your customer and mentally walk through each step of the experience. What do you want to happen? How do you want to think and feel? Write it down.

Now that you've defined your customers' experience at every touchpoint, be sure to recognize and reward your staffers who provide outstanding quality service and products.

Tom talked about one of the ways his company recognizes actions he wants to encourage: "As long as we take care of the customer, we get repeat business. So we recognize our employees with 'Caught taking care of the customer' certificates. They display them, but we also keep a copy in their files and we go over them when they have their reviews. It keeps them motivated, and they should be rewarded."

Embrace mistakes

Creating a culture around service and quality doesn't mean punishing mistakes. They will happen and it's better to accept and try to solve them rather than ignore them. (Or worse, to train your employees to hide mistakes!)

In one of my interviews, Rick, the owner of an event venue, told me that they not only encourage employees to talk about their mistakes, they actually reward staffers for coming clean about errors. At quarterly management meetings, employees were asked to describe a mistake they had made, how much it cost the company, and ways to resolve or prevent it from happening again. This multiplied each employee's experience level because they all learned from each other's mistakes.

Screen hires for service

If you want your employees to create a service-driven culture, it's important to hire people who are wired that way.

The behavioral interviewing questions I mentioned in Chapter 7 will help you get a glimpse of the candidate's personality. Here's a perfect example: "Tell me about a time when you had to handle a situation with a difficult client. What was the situation, and how did you handle it?"

You're looking for clues in the answer to identify attitudes and previous experience. Signs of empathy, ownership, and initiative point to strong customer service aptitude. Judgmental behavior, blaming or "not my problem" attitudes are warning signs that you should look elsewhere for your new hire.

When it comes to your existing staff, to get serious about quality and service standards in your business, quickly identify those who don't fit your culture and encourage them to move on.

At Jason's language learning software company, cultural fit is non-negotiable. He says, "I believe everybody here is intrinsically motivated to do what they're doing."

His company boasts a 90% repurchase rate among its customers. That percentage could grow even higher. During our interview, he commented ruefully that the company just didn't have additional products to sell to some buyers.

Dr. Jeff, an orthopedist with his own successful practice, hires employees who share his drive and desire for continuous improvement. "I'm driven by an intense desire to achieve perfection. That means that the care I give in my practice needs to be better than anyone else. I'm always analyzing how I can improve, and I need staff to be that way too. We have a facility that's unlike anyplace else. But I told my staff that we still have to provide a service experience and care that's a thousand times better than the environment. To provide the best care, you have to stay cutting-edge."

Paul, the founder of a payroll service, describes his company culture as "very customer/client-centric." He says, "We see ourselves as partners with our customers and not just vendors. It is our goal to create stable long-term relationships with them."

Paul's company relies on an assessment tool to select candidates with the skills and personality that fit the organization's goals: "We use the Predictive Index survey to make sure that we hire the right people with the right skills. The message is, 'pay attention to detail and get it right.'"

The Predictive Index is an assessment that measures people's work-related personality. When you know how a candidate scores on four spectrums – assertive, people-oriented, patient, and structured – you can match the right personality with the right position. Your employees will be much happier and more successful, and so will your business.

Make it easy to give good service

When you've got the right employees in place, document and review processes to ensure they lead to quality service and products, not hinder them. Give your people latitude to use their own judgment when solving customer issues. Don't make them cite "company policy" as a reason not to solve a problem.

"We empower our employees to make decisions at the closest point of contact. That allows us to really impact what's happening with our customers," says Micky, CEO of a manufacturing company.

While you're at it, make the financial commitment to keep up with equipment and technology improvements that will ensure the creation of quality products and service. You can use high-tech solutions such as a CRM combined with low-tech solutions like a database or simple filing system to create a system that makes your customer feel that they are special to your company.

Solicit and act on feedback

Bob and Cathy continuously improve their custom cleaning business and do whatever they can to generate word-of-mouth recommendations from happy customers. After each interaction, they give the customer a satisfaction survey and act on every comment to reach their goal of 100% customer satisfaction. Cathy said, "If there's an issue, it's 100% resolved. Even minor things that aren't a big deal – we just get them taken care of immediately."

I asked Terry, CEO of a consulting and engineering firm specializing in cost recovery, to name the top reason that his business was able to survive and thrive during the recession while so many others closed. His answer? "Deliver service so well that we get referrals."

When in doubt, give more

There are many factors that influence a customer's decision to do business with your company. True loyalty is based on your continuous delivery of superior value. Loyal customers drive sustainable profits and growth, so it makes economic sense to give a little more than your competitors to keep a customer.

The thriving leaders I interviewed used superior value to beat out competitors for new customers and to retain profitable existing relationships.

Lance, president of a $1.8-million company that provides computer technology and services, shared one of his recession survival strategies: "Everyone in our organization became more available to all clients, 24/7, at all levels."

Commercial heating and plumbing supply company CEO Verbon also followed the "give more" strategy to fend off competition during the downturn. The company offered additional services at cost. While competitors charged fees, they gave diagrams, laid out systems, and gave plans for free.

Describing the impact of the recession on business, Richard said of his specialty manufacturing and engineering company, "We cut back the workforce but kept up communication with customers. We went out and got every job. We didn't lose a job because of price."

Partnership and performance pay off

Tom could teach his own master class on business success principles:

> *First, you have to know who your customer is. Once you know that, you have to figure out what's preventing them from fulfilling their goals. If you offer a solution that meets that need, you can then partner with them in success. It makes them look good to their customer, and in turn, they keep coming back to us with additional opportunities.*

Tom has a competitive disadvantage – his company performs 95% of its work out of state. His competitors, local companies, don't incur travel costs. That forces him to get creative. "One way we found to outperform our competitors," he said, "is to have our teams use checklists for steps of the project. Those must be performed perfectly." He commissioned his own custom software for his team members to check off steps and send photo documentation. And his number-one tip? "Hire employees who are overachievers."

Customer service and quality aren't the sexy elements of business. But for your small business, they can make the difference between survival and oblivion. Increased service levels and outstanding product offerings helped our Super Owners outlast the economic challenge.

CHAPTER SUMMARY
Give, Then Give Some More

Key Points

Success Code, Principle #8: Successful business owners who truly understand "survival skills" know how to hold onto customers with increased service levels, how to provide outstanding product and service offerings, and how to stay in front of the emerging needs of potential new customers.

- By giving more now, you ensure the long-term success of your company.

- Customer service is a business differentiator.

- Delivering outstanding service is more difficult with social networks, online review sites, and instant communication tools, but companies can reap huge rewards when they wow customers with great service.

- Poor service and inferior products cost companies revenue, affect reputation, squeeze profits, and limit growth. It can even kill companies.

- If your business has a higher percentage of repeat customers than your competitors, then you likely have a lower average customer acquisition cost, and that equals a competitive advantage.

- Businesses with poor products and services often haven't empowered employees to be part of the solution.

- To have a culture of customer service, it must apply to every employee in the organization, not just those with "customer service representative" as a title.

- The most successful small business leaders believe that the practice *most responsible* for their success was their renewed focus on the customer.

- As the owner, you have to provide outstanding service to your *team* as well as your *customers*.

- The key to developing proper customer standards and training is carefully considering the experience your customers have at every touchpoint.

- Give your people latitude to use their own judgment when solving customer issues.

- Thriving leaders used superior value to beat out competitors for new customers and to retain profitable existing relationships.

CHAPTER 9

Never Stop Learning

Knowledge is power. We've all heard that old chestnut, but successful owners embrace it. They understand that learning may not seem "urgent," but without it they cannot keep their company in the forefront of their industry and ahead of their competitors. They also know that keeping up with business and industry skills is not only critical to success, but it's also very motivating and something everyone can use when times are tougher. The important steps are to find ways to enjoy learning, encourage company participation, and follow through consistently.

Know what you need to know

You don't know everything about business or even your own industry. It's impossible to keep pace with the new information that's created daily. Population growth, advances in technology and science – they all create an ever-increasing amount of information. In 2010, *The Economist* noted, "Between 1990 and 2005, more than one billion people worldwide entered the middle class. As they get richer, they become more literate, which fuels information growth. The amount of digital information increases tenfold every five years."[1]

It's enough to make small business owners want to retreat to bed and hide under the covers! But there's good news: you don't *need* to know everything.

However, what you *must* do is continue to learn in order to continue to grow. Increasing competition, rising customer demands, and business cycles require that you continuously upgrade your own skills, as well as those of your staff. As a business owner, if you're not constantly

---

[1] http://www.economist.com/node/15557443

educating yourself on new methods and technology, you'll miss out on time and money-saving ideas that keep your business competitive.

I mentioned in earlier chapters that consumers now wield much more power in this global economy than they did one hundred years ago. With unlimited choice come high standards. To find your customers, understand their expectations, and meet them profitably, you must invest in continuous learning.

Your business survival depends on it.

One cautionary note about continuous learning: you need to have knowledge, but that knowledge also needs to be applied. Don't fall into the trap of waiting to take action on ideas until you learn more. All the knowledge in the world is useless if it's not applied. You must take *action*.

Here's the winning formula I learned from the Super Owners I studied: learn, apply, measure, and adjust.

What's Broken

Until the early 19th century, buying new clothes, new curtains, or new bed covers was a luxury limited to the wealthy. It took skilled weavers weeks to make bespoke cloth, which was then sent to seamstresses who spent more weeks cutting and sewing. Those who could not afford to pay the wages of a skilled artisan had to make do with castoffs or rely on their own ingenuity to remake old garments.

Then along came the Industrial Revolution, when inventors created machines like power looms that promised to save labor and increase productivity in the textile industry. But not everyone rejoiced. A group of English textile artisans called the Luddites protested these new devices, fearing that their personal work would be replaced by low-wage unskilled laborers using machines. For two years, handloom weavers burned mills and machinery, destroying many before the British government suppressed the movement. And guess what happened? Over time, lower skilled laborers using machines *did* replace the hand weavers.

The lesson here is clear: *learning and innovation transforms industries.* Ignoring or railing against advancements can't stop change. Companies whose staff suffers from "we've always done it this way" attitudes stagnate. More flexible organizations take advantage of industry trends and new technology, leaving those resistant to change with an ever-shrinking share of the market.

Being unaware or unwilling to try new ideas impacts every part of your business. Let's assess the potential damage.

Missing the big customer shifts

Without continuous learning, a business loses touch with its customers and what they need. Competitors swoop in, luring clients and prospects to buy from them instead.

Think of how many retailers missed the shift in customer shopping habits from in-store to online that started in the late 1990s and took off in the 2000s. Entire companies were made or crushed by that change.

Stale products, sour customers

Without constant learning, it's hard to come up with new ideas. Your products suffer. Even industry-leading organizations can fall victim to stasis. Internet giant Yahoo once dominated the web universe, providing a high-traffic portal for web searching, news, and communications. After leading the market for several years, Yahoo began losing ground to upstart Google, which invested heavily in developing new features and services to attract the growing online population. Today, Yahoo seems to be on an upswing, having doubled down on product development following the hire of top Google staffer Marissa Mayer.

One of my interviewees, Bill, the president of a business-to-business telecommunications company, sums up the never-ending challenge that small business owners face: "Business is shifting rapidly. It's tough to stay in front of the changes."

Stuck in the echo chamber

How do you know when your knowledge is stale? One clue is that your company has become a "me too" organization – one that markets, sells, and operates exactly like all your competitors.

The culprit is the lack of a broader perspective. It's impossible to discover new ideas if all your attention is focused within your own industry and on your own competitors. As with Henry Ford and the moving assembly line, the concepts that propel a company to 10 or 100 times growth typically aren't as much innovative as they are ideas borrowed from other industries.

Marketing suffers

Without continuous learning, your business can suffer from marketing myopia. Tactics that worked 10 years ago no longer bring leads or sales, but your company continues to pour money into them because you haven't kept up on changes. If your company spends tens of thousands of dollars on trade show attendance even when the strategy doesn't work just because you've "always gone," you're not using your marketing dollars effectively.

The last decade has spurred huge shifts in marketing strategies and tools. Social media and plummeting costs of technology put small businesses on an even playing field with Fortune 500 companies. But if you're not taking advantage of the new tools, you'll find yourself losing ground to competitors…like those retailers who missed the shift to e-commerce.

Employee attrition

Another danger of not learning? Employees who aren't advancing their knowledge and growing their skills become bored. Then frustrated. Finally, they leave to find new challenges and opportunities.

I see this often. One of the benefits I offer my clients is running group-hiring meetings with them. We post ads for open positions within client organizations and interview the applicants together. Early in the interview, I ask every applicant why he or she is looking for a new job. Nearly all of them cite a lack of challenge in their current position. They want to learn and grow, but aren't getting the opportunities to do so.

Companies ignore employee discontent at their own peril. Turnover rates will accelerate as the Millennial generation – who value training and development highly – makes up an ever-higher percentage of the workforce.

When competitors' offerings are more appealing than yours, it's a clue to examine your organization's learning practices. Do employees have the tools, time, and motivation they need to help create marketplace advantages? If not, where can you fill in the gaps?

Today's higher education institutions don't prepare the students with the skills that businesses need. The savvy business owner doesn't rail at this gap and do nothing; she finds ways to get her employees the skills she needs to grow her business.

Your brain shrinks when you stop learning

When you stop learning, your brain changes. While it doesn't physically shrink, you do lose some of your cognitive ability. The physicality of your brain changes; you can no longer learn as well. This atrophy affects your ability to strategize and brainstorm new ideas.

But there is good news – reading improves your brain's structure and function by stimulating certain parts:

> In a six-month daily reading program from Carnegie Mellon, scientists discovered that the volume of white matter in the language area of the brain actually increased. Further, they showed that brain structure can be improved with this training, making it more important than ever to adopt a healthy love of reading.[2]

The benefits of reading get even better. Not only does reading improve your brain function, but reading about a new idea or experience is almost as good as actually experiencing it. When we read, our brain doesn't distinguish between reading about an experience and actually having the experience. The same neurological regions are stimulated, whether reading or experiencing it.[3] This is why elite-level athletes all spend a portion of their training time visualizing their playing routines – it improves performance.

I'm learning, so what's the problem?

Owners may feel stimulated because they make frequent decisions and learn new ideas through executing the business. But they don't notice that employees – stuck performing the same activities, day after day – are feeling stagnant.

---

[2] http://oedb.org/ilibrarian/your-brain-on-books-10-things-that-happen-to-our-minds-when-we-read/

[3] http://www.nytimes.com/2012/03/18/opinion/sunday/the-neuroscience-of-your-brain-on-fiction.html

Employee training and development has been on a decline, perhaps because of the recession. Apprenticeship programs are harder to find, as well as management training programs. This shortage of opportunities to learn on the job helps explain the increase in popularity of unpaid internships.

Why It's Broken

It's easy to blame "information overload" as a reason to forgo learning. There's so much to know! How can you tell where to start, what to read or watch, who to believe? Twenty-four-hour news channels, social media, blog posts, instant messages, texts, email. Magazines, newsletters, reports, books. It's impossible to absorb it all. But ignoring the deluge isn't the answer to overwhelm.

Understanding your customers' challenges and goals, keeping up with new strategies and technology – these are essential to running a profitable business. The most successful CEOs I interviewed were able to maintain the tightrope challenge of *doing work* while carving out time to continue to *learn* about work. They made it a priority.

Others – those who were profitable with moderate effort during the boom years – never developed the discipline of continuous learning. Success lulled them into believing that they would continue to be profitable, come what may. When the recession hit, the complacent owners were hit hardest. Without new ideas, they lost market share to businesses whose owners continuously built their knowledge of strategy, operations, marketing, sales, technology and the customer.

Let's take a closer look at the reasons why even well-intentioned business owners lose their learning mojo.

Myth of no time

According to conventional wisdom, modern adults are busier today than at any other time in history. Television talk shows, magazines, and websites burst with advice on how to manage stress and "find more time."

But I've got shocking news for you. It turns out that it's just not true. Americans today actually work *less* and enjoy *more* leisure time than they did in the 1960s. Po Bronson writes in *Time* magazine:

> If life seems more rushed than ever, you might be surprised to learn that we Americans don't have less leisure time than we did 40 years ago. We actually have more leisure time, and quite a bit more. What counts as leisure is up for argument, but under every definition the numbers have gone up. We get about 45 minutes a day of extra leisure.[4]

The U.S. Bureau of Labor Statistics, which publishes the annual *American Time Use Survey*, reports that we enjoyed an average of five hours and 22 minutes of leisure time per day in 2012. So where does it go? For starters, we spent two hours and 50 minutes of that free time watching television.[5]

Reading is dead

In the What's Broken section of this chapter, I talked about the positive effects of reading on brain function. Yet fewer and fewer people seem to be reading books. As an avid reader myself, these statistics pain me:

- One-third of high school graduates never read another book for the rest of their lives.

- 42% of college graduates never read another book after college.

- 80% of U.S. families did not buy or read a book last year.

---

[4] How We Spend Our Leisure Time - TIME - http://content.time.com/time/nation/article/0,8599,1549394,00.html#ixzz2mjMwkeB4

[5] http://www.bls.gov/news.release/atus.nr0.htm

- 70% of U.S. adults have not been in a bookstore in the last five years.
- 57% of new books are not read to completion.
  (Source: The Jenkins Group, 2003)[6]

Not only is reading less popular today than a century ago, the rising popularity of smart phones and tablets gives us our "screen" fix anytime, anywhere. The ability to jump from app to app, plug in to social media, or give ourselves the "sugar rush" of playing an online game can make reading feel challenging and even boring by comparison. Why exercise the brain when you can be entertained?

In 2010, Americans spent two hours and 35 minutes online and an average of 50 minutes on mobile devices every day. Add that to the time spent watching television (note that some folks are juggling two screens at once). Is it any wonder we can't find time to read?

Scarred by school

For some business owners, the high school and college experience was so scarring, they'll avoid ever picking up a book again. I can sympathize – plowing through dull textbooks is enough to turn a person off reading for a lifetime.

With others, learning disabilities make reading extensively an impossible feat. Studies have shown that a high percentage of entrepreneurs show signs of dyslexia – as high as 35% in the U.S. But famous names like Kinko's founder Paul Orfalea, Charles Schwab, Richard Branson, and Cisco Systems CEO John Chambers prove that dyslexia doesn't rule out major success in business. In fact, Julie Logan, a professor of entrepreneurship at Cass Business School in London, believes there's a strong connection between the skills that students

---

[6] http://mentalfloss.com/article/27590/who-reads-books

with learning disabilities develop to cope and the entrepreneurial traits that make them effective business owners.[8]

A December 2007 article on Bloomberg's BusinessWeek.com summed it up this way: "The ability to grasp the big picture, persistence, and creativity are a few of the entrepreneurial traits of many dyslexics."[9]

Tyranny of the urgent

I've said it over and over – we business owners are busy people. With all the priorities competing for your time, you might think that you can't possibly spend your time or your team's time reading. Or surfing the Internet. Or going to training seminars when there's so darned much work to be done here at the office!

You're not the only one who thinks this way. An article in the *Journal of Small Business and Enterprise Management* (2007) tells us: "The reason often cited for the poor relationship between small businesses and their uptake of vocational education and training is that small business owner-managers claim that they are too busy to engage in training or any type of learning activity."[10]

Here's my own experience with the "too busy to learn" syndrome: at my quarterly leadership summit, we take one day to work on our business – masterminding with other owners and planning for the next quarter. It's incredibly powerful, and my clients credit those focused days with major increases in revenue, free time and peace of mind. Yet, each quarter, a few business owners tell me that while they *know*

---

[8] http://www.amanet.org/training/articles/New-Research-Reveals-Many-Entrepreneurs-Are-Dyslexic.aspx

[9] http://www.businessweek.com/stories/2007-12-12/why-dyslexics-make-great-entrepreneursbusinessweek-business-news-stock-market-and-financial-advice

[10] Elizabeth Walker, Janice Redmond, Beverley Webster, Megan Le Clus, (2007) "Small business owners: too busy to train?", Journal of Small Business and Enterprise Development, Vol. 14 Iss: 2, pp.294 - 306

participating in the summits would really help their business, they "just can't get out of the office for the day." Sadly, they remain stuck, year after year.

The guilt factor

When everyone at your organization is visibly working hard, it's difficult to justify taking time out to learn. Reading a book, watching a video, or taking a class doesn't feel like real work. It's natural; we unconsciously value what looks like action over passive learning in a business setting. And what would your staff think if they saw you? And how can you expect your team to pick up the slack while you're off at a conference?

Paralysis by analysis

While there are business owners who've vowed never to read another book or take another class, business owners who love studying, researching, and absorbing new ideas really do exist. And among that group are a few who get caught in the endless quest for "perfect knowledge." They think, "I'll get around to launching this new product (or implementing this new idea) just as soon as I do a little more research."

Decisions aren't made. Plans aren't executed. The owner is trapped in an endless loop of learning and learning, but never doing. Information by itself will not make a business more profitable – *only information that's put into action.*

Systems

In a learning free-for-all, the benefits are limited. When business owners *do* carve out time for learning and advancing skills, they don't always have the systems in place to squeeze the maximum value from the effort. Nobody's in charge and there's no strategy around it.

There's no method for disseminating information among the team members. Who needs to know what? When? How will they share the new information with their team or the rest of the company, if it's applicable? One person may attend a conference, take a class, or read about a groundbreaking new concept, but if that information isn't shared, only a small part of the potential advantage is realized.

As part of my coaching programs, I give a subscription to *Success* magazine to each of my clients. It's a stellar publication – the perfect combination of information and inspiration, designed specifically for entrepreneurs. Even though I strongly suggest that my clients share it with their staff members (who could use information and inspiration, too), the magazine usually sits on their desk, gathering dust.

Burned out

Business owners who've pushed themselves too hard can reach a breaking point. They're burned out. The last thing they want to do is take a class, read a book, or study a new topic. But interestingly, learning something new could be the spark you need to burn off burnout. Learning involves new stimuli and experiences. These stimuli and experiences cause new neurons to form.

"When people are intensely engaged in doing and learning new things, their well-being and happiness can blossom," says a *US News & World Report's Money* article, "Why Learning Leads to Happiness."[11]

Feeling exposed

Business owners are self-made. To build a business from nothing, they've had to be self-reliant. This makes many of them reluctant to reveal deficiencies in their own knowledge.

---

[11] http://money.usnews.com/money/personal-finance/articles/2012/04/10/why-learning-leads-to-happiness

Economist Steven Levitt, co-author of the best-selling book, *Freakonomics, A Rogue Economist Explores the Hidden Side of Everything* (Turtleback, 2009), points out the danger of this attitude:

> What I've found in business is that almost no one will ever admit to not knowing the answer to a question… And I've found it's really one of the most destructive factors in business – is that everyone masquerades like they know the answer and no one will ever admit they don't know the answer, and it makes it almost impossible to learn.[12]

Ego bound

Successful business owners are often mavericks who have forged their own way against tremendous odds. With that success can come hubris. They doubt that another individual – particularly one who isn't in their own industry or vastly more successful than they are – has anything of value to offer.

Wasted investment

Fear of wasted investment stops some small business owners from funding training and learning opportunities for their staff. Worried that their time and resources will only benefit another business when the employee jumps ship, owners stop paying for training or providing time off.

The president of a 200-person civil engineering firm headquartered in southeast Michigan brushed off his HR manager's request for skills training for staff with comments like these: "Why should I pay for them to take a class? Employees should learn new skills on their own time. It shows initiative." Or, "I only invest in people who show me that they invest in themselves first."

---

[12] http:// freakonomics.com/2012/01/04/why-is-%E2%80%9Ci-don%E2%80%99t-know%E2%80%9D-so-hard-to-say-a-new-freakonomics-radio-podcast/

The president feared that if he paid for his employees to learn new skills, it would not only negatively impact billable hours, but that employees would view paid training as an entitlement rather than a reward. His biggest concern was that the company would pay for a training or certification for an employee who would immediately use those new qualifications to snag a better job at another company.

That president isn't alone in his attitude. Many small business owners refuse to send employees to conferences or trade shows to gain business knowledge because they fear that the spending will be wasted. Visions of pleasure jaunts and heavy drinking trump the promise of any business value.

What Will Fix It

Excuses for not learning are abundant: lack of time, lack of resources, lack of motivation. But there's a fear that should spur your desire to keep advancing your knowledge and skills: lack of business.

Training and development for yourself and your staff is the single most important growth strategy that a business can have in this competitive and fast-changing world. Dr. Laith, who owns a high-growth orthopedic center, places a high value on learning in his practice. He attends at least one major conference per year and says his team is "always looking for new ways to use technology." He believes that "you've got to constantly re-invent yourself." He fuels his reinvention by reading journals and talking with innovative colleagues around the country.

By investing in continuous learning – both financially and with time – you'll enjoy greater success, more personal satisfaction, and have happier, more productive employees.

Find the time

Bemoaning our lack of time isn't the answer. Other business owners face the same time constraints we have, yet they manage to continuously grow their skills. Richard Branson, Oprah Winfrey, Bill Gates – we all juggle the same 24 hours.

The trick isn't having more time; it's *making* more time. It's doing a better job of organizing the time you have. It's eliminating the things that suck time out of your day – like meetings, email, and television. Delegate responsibilities so that others in our organization have the chance to grow, and you have time to learn something new.

Free and low-cost learning resources are everywhere

If you view learning as something that takes place only in a classroom, you could be missing out on opportunities to get cutting-edge training for free or at low cost. Any small business owner who doesn't embrace continuous learning runs the risk of having the business stagnate and lose competitiveness. Fortunately, these days there are more inexpensive resources than ever before for learning new information that will help you grow your business.

From quick YouTube videos on "how to" topics to intense graduate school-level courses, the Internet is serving up new ways to learn almost anything. The prestigious Massachusetts Institute of Technology (MIT) led the revolution by posting all of its coursework online for free. Here are three other online opportunities:

- **Coursera** (coursera.com) is an organization partnering with more than 100 universities to offer massive open online courses (MOOCs) via video, available for free or at a low cost. More than five million people have enrolled in these MOOCs.

- **Khan Academy** (khanacademy.com) is a non-profit educational website created by educator Salman Khan, a graduate of MIT and Harvard Business School. His mission is to provide a "free world-class education for anyone, anywhere." The website features 700+ video tutorials teaching finance, economics, macroeconomics, microeconomics, computer science, physics, astronomy, mathematics, healthcare, history, medicine, biology, chemistry, and American civics.

- **TED Talks** are video presentations delivered by leading experts and innovative thinkers from all walks of life. You can watch these videos for free at www.ted.com. Topics include business, science, the arts, and global issues. These short videos – three to 18 minutes – will inspire you and rekindle your passion for achievement.

In addition to their typical foundation-level courses for transfer students, local community colleges offer workshops and non-credit courses for small business owners. Many also provide networking opportunities, counseling, and mentoring, often at no cost at all.

Chambers of Commerce and economic development organizations offer classes, seminars, workshops, and speakers on business-related topics. Most are very low-cost.

Business networking groups often host speakers who are subject matter experts. In 30 to 90 minutes, you can learn about new marketing tools, types of funding for your business, how to hire better, or how to reduce insurance costs.

Your library houses thousands of business books and magazines, yours for the borrowing. And if your local library doesn't have a title you want, the librarian can often request it from another library in the

network. Many libraries even have access to electronic books now –
just load a digital book onto your Kindle or Nook and learn on the go.

Associations exist to provide their members with a competitive
advantage. They offer free and discounted training opportunities
and resource materials on topics that are directly applicable to your
business. You could learn a lot simply from talking with your fellow
members and learning from their experiences.

Bob and Cathy, husband and wife owners of a carpet cleaning
business, credit their association with helping them stay on top of
the latest techniques, methods, and tips in their industry. They take
advantage of their association's newsletters, classes, and website.

Alan, the CEO of a $5-million company that manufactures specialized
machinery for the automotive industry, turns to his association for
education: "We stay up on what's happening in the state, as well as
the Michigan Economic Development Corporation and the Michigan
Manufacturers Association. We attend seminars, read overviews,
trends, websites and books."

My clients, Lynne and Rich, own a window cleaning company,
and they credit the International Window Cleaning Association
with teaching them industry best practices, steering them toward
significant company growth.

Learn outside your industry, too

When it comes to learning and development, don't rely *only* on your
own industry. If you do, you might miss the ideas that could propel
growth. Learn from other industries to create innovative ideas in your
own business.

Steve, the chief operations officer of a business-to-business telecommunications company, uses industry and outside resources to combat challenges. "It's tough to stay in front of the changes involving equipment, maintenance plans, service level agreements," he says. "We share ideas with non-competitors."

Paul, founder of the rapidly growing payroll processing company, agrees: "We attend conferences and go outside of our industry a lot. We also have reached out to higher education to remain cutting-edge in data management."

Read and read some more

Diane, a home medical supply company owner, believes in the business-boosting power of reading. She says, "We use resource material for the industry, such as trade magazines. I read a lot about business and relate it back to mine."

Super Owner Tom *spends 25% of his time reading.* He's absorbing information and ideas on his own industry as well as those of his clients, so he knows exactly what challenges they face and can solve them better than any competitor.

Vendor-powered training

Similar to associations arming its members with competitive advantages, vendors can help their customers with education.

One of the major reasons that John's $1-million floor covering business held steady during the recession was education. He told me, "We attend Mohawk University at least once a year and educate the customer to build a relationship with them." Mohawk, the world's largest floor covering company, provides classroom training, online training, and other resources to its retailers, giving them a competitive advantage over retailers of other manufacturers. Training includes product knowledge and installation information as well as leadership development, sales growth, social media, and business management. Mohawk understands that providing its retailers with more knowledge is the key to increasing sales of the company's own products.

Now that you're armed with a bevy of free and low-cost learning resources, let's tackle a few of the emotional challenges that stop business owners from growing their own skills and knowledge.

Be okay with feeling dumb

In your business, often you're the one that employees go to for answers. To admit that you don't know everything and ask for others to teach you can feel humbling. But if you adopt a growth mindset, you'll understand that when you're developing a new skill or learning about a new topic, it's natural to feel incompetent. That is, until you learn the new thing – and then you'll feel competent.

"We look at technologies on the Internet and talk to suppliers. We're not afraid to try new things," said Jim, president of a plastics extrusion manufacturing concern, describing how his company stays ahead in a highly competitive industry.

Don't go it alone! Coaching and mentors can help

As business owners, we can feel like lone wolves, battling enemies and the elements on our own. Having an advocate in your corner can give you a competitive advantage and inject renewed energy into the business, intellectually and emotionally. That's why business coaches and mentors are often the secret weapons of the most successful business owners.

Coaching isn't paying someone to tell you what to do. *Harvard Business Review* (1996) says, "The goal of coaching is the goal of good management: to make the most of an organization's valuable resources."[13] Successful leaders hire business professionals (please check those qualifications before you hire) whose advice and counsel can more quickly advance business growth and profitability than they could by themselves.

According to a 2001 study by *The Manchester Review* reported in *Fortune* magazine, "Training alone improved leadership skills by 22%. When combined with business coaching, the improvement jumped to 77%."[14]

In your coach or mentor, you have a resource to assess and focus on specific situations as they unfold. It's just-in-time learning, encouragement, and a new way of looking at things when you need it.

Richard, who heads a 25-person specialty manufacturing and engineering firm, is an early adopter of the latest technology. His organization has been moving toward video training to continuously grow his staff's skills. When I asked him the reasons that his company managed to do well during the recession, he said that he turned to older, more experienced mentors: "We want to stay as nimble and flexible as we can."

Spread the learning

Remember at the beginning of this chapter when I said that training and development for you and your staff is the single most important growth strategy that a business can have? We've just covered the importance of business owners learning and developing. It's equally important to keep *your staff* learning continuously and sharing that information. Your business will benefit from new ideas, increased

---

[13] http://hbr.org/1996/11/the-executive-as-coach/ib

[14] Maximizing the Impact of Executive Coaching The Return Investment of Executive Coaching, Behavioral Change, Organizational Outcomes and Return on Investment, The Manchester Review, 2001

engagement, higher productivity, and lower turnover. Isn't that an investment worth making?

To achieve the full benefits of learning among your team, find the people in your organization who love to learn and make them your teachers. Jason moved a staffer to a research and intelligence role in his language learning company because "she recognized the need for the information and had the passion to follow through." She keeps the entire company up to date on new trends in the industry and what the competition is doing.

Tom has an internship program that brings the brightest young people into his company, where they keep the established workers up-to-date on the latest technology advancements.

Paul believes that learning and development gives his payroll processing company a competitive advantage. He's proud that his company boasts the highest number of Certified Payroll Professionals (CPPs) in the industry.

To make it stick, create a system

Investing in continuous learning for you and your staff is a commitment of significant resources – time and money. Maximize that investment by creating ways to share new ideas and information among your entire organization.

For personal use, apps like Evernote or Instapaper let you capture and store articles from websites to read later, offline.

If you plan to curate content to share with your staff, remember that access is as important as the content itself. The easier it is to find and use the information, the more likely your employees will engage with it and benefit from it.

Assess your current state: does everyone in the organization know what resources already exist? How about where those resources are located? And how to access them? Options can be dead simple, like routing magazines, newsletters, and periodicals around the organization, where recipients read the material, check off their name, and route it to the next person on the list.

Company or department meetings are a prime opportunity for employees to share information they've learned *and* improve their presentation skills at the same time.

Digital tools like wikis (a web application that allows people to add, modify, or delete content in collaboration with others), knowledge bases, and intranets let you share information with your staff electronically.

You can buy off-the-shelf tools like LiveBinders.com that let you organize digital resources such as images, documents, PDFs, presentations, and videos into virtual three-ring binders that your staff can access.

I structure my quarterly leadership summits as company development days for my clients. I bring in a thought-leading speaker to teach my clients a timely topic. Summit attendees spend the day in various mini-workshops, broadening their knowledge, while they work on their business plans for the next 90 days.

Make it easy

The goal is to disseminate new information as easily as possible in a way that employees will actually use. Finding methods that work for your company will encourage all staffers to take advantage of the information. Don't be afraid to try different tools and approaches, and when you find something that works, stick with it.

Make it fun

There are thousands of ways to learn new ideas and improve your skills, but you may not follow through with anything that's too complicated, challenging, or forces you to change your normal routine drastically. The secret to making learning stick is to find ways to make it enjoyable. Learning doesn't have to be a chore; it can be more like play. For young children, playing is the way that they learn the most fundamental skills and ideas of their lives, such as how to communicate and how to walk.

Flex your brain by learning

Take this advice gathered from scientists and business owners:

- From the Franklin Institute for Science Learning: "Consider your brain a muscle, and find opportunities to flex it."[15]

- "Read, read, read," says Dr. Amir Soas of Case Western Reserve University Medical School in Cleveland.[16]

- "Challenging the brain is crucial to building up more 'cognitive reserve' to counter brain-damaging disease," says Dr. David Bennett of Chicago's Rush University.[17]

- Super Owner interviewee Verbon agrees, "To stay in business, you have to keep up with your knowledge."

Find ways to enjoy learning, and encourage everyone in your company to participate. Make the new information easy to find and easy to share. Your business and your brain will thank you for it!

---

[15] http://www.fi.edu/learn/brain/exercise.html

[16, 17] Scientists: Brain Use Slows Deterioration, http://abcnews.go.com/Health/story?id=118119

CHAPTER SUMMARY
Never Stop Learning

Key Points

Success Code, Principle #9: Super Owner recession survivors practice continuous learning to keep their company in the forefront of their industry and ahead of their competitors.

- Increasing competition, rising customer demands, and business cycles require that you continuously upgrade your own skills, as well as those of your staff.

- All the knowledge in the world is useless if it's not applied. You must take action.

- Here's the winning formula I learned from the Super Owners I studied: learn, apply, measure, and adjust.

- Learning and innovation transforms industries. Ignoring or railing against advancements can't stop change. Without continuous learning, a business loses touch with its customers and what they need.

- It's impossible to discover new ideas if all your attention is focused within your own industry and on your own competitors.

- Employees who are looking for a new job often cite a lack of challenge in their current position. They want to learn and grow, but aren't getting the opportunities to do so.

- Reading improves your brain function, and reading about a new idea or experience is almost as good as actually experiencing it.

- The most successful CEOs I interviewed were able to maintain the tightrope challenge of doing work while carving out time to continue to learn about work.

- Information by itself will not make a business more profitable – only information that's put into action.

- Learning something new could be the spark you need to burn off burnout. Learning involves new stimuli and experiences that cause new neurons to form.

- Training and development for yourself and your staff is the single most important growth strategy that a business can have in this competitive and fast-changing world.

- There are more inexpensive resources than ever before for learning new information that will help you grow your business.

- Vendors can help their customers with education.

- To admit that you don't know everything and ask for others to teach you can feel humbling. But if you adopt a growth mindset, you'll understand that when you're developing a new skill or learning about a new topic, it's natural to feel incompetent until you learn the new thing.

- Having an advocate can give you a competitive advantage and inject renewed energy into the business.

- The easier it is to find and use the information, the more likely your employees will engage with it and benefit from it.

- The secret to making learning stick is to find ways to make it enjoyable. Learning doesn't have to be a chore; it can be more like play.

Notes

Chapter 1

1. "SBA Office of Advocacy: Frequently Asked Questions (PDF)." U.S. Small Business Administration. U.S. Small Business Administration, Sept. 2012. Web. 9 Jan. 2014.

2. Morales, Lymari. "Self-Employed Workers Clock the Most Hours Each Week." Self-Employed Workers Clock the Most Hours Each Week. Gallup, 26 Aug. 2009. Web. 08 Jan. 2014.

3. Nery, Kevin A., CBB, CBI, M&AMI. "Burnout Is Often the Reason for Selling a Business." SouthCoastToday.com. Southcoast Business Bulletin, 13 Jan. 2013. Web. 08 Jan. 2014.

Chapter 2

1. Warren Buffet and the Interpretation of Financial Statements, Mary Buffett, David Clark, Simon & Schuster, 2011, preface.

2. Atkinson, Robert D., Luke A. Stewart, Scott M. Andes, and Stephen Ezell. "Worse Than the Great Depression: What the Experts Are Missing About American Manufacturing Decline | The Information Technology & Innovation Foundation." The Information Technology & Innovation Foundation, 19 Mar. 2012. Web. 08 Jan. 2014.

3. Klein, Karen E. "What's Behind High Business Failure Rates?" BusinessWeek.com. Bloomberg BusinessWeek, 30 Sept. 1999. Web. 8 Jan. 2014.

4. Carney, Karen. "Swipe These Critical Numbers!" Inc.com. Inc., 11 Dec. 1999. Web. 08 Jan. 2014.

Chapter 3

1. Prive, Tanya. "Top 32 Quotes Every Entrepreneur Should Live By." Forbes. Forbes Magazine, 02 May 2013. Web. 08 Jan. 2014.

2. Michael, Paul. "17 Things Car Salesmen Don't Want You to Know." Wise Bread. Killer Aces Media, 13 Mar. 2013. Web. 08 Jan. 2014.

3. Website of BrianSolis.com. http://www.briansolis.com/about/. Web. 08 Jan. 2014

4. Solis, Brian. "Digital Darwinism: What Killed Borders, Blockbuster and Polaroid and How to Survive." LinkedIn.com. LinkedIn, 27 Feb. 2013. Web. 08 Jan. 2014.

5. Fredrickson B. L. (2004). The broaden-and-build theory of positive emotions. Philos. Trans. R. Soc. Lond. B Biol. Sci. 359, 1367–1378.10.1098/rstb.2004.1512

6. Roubini, Nouriel. "The Impact Of Chrysler's Bankruptcy." Forbes. Forbes Magazine, 7 May 2009. Web. 08 Jan. 2014.

7. "Sudden Wealth Syndrome (SWS)." Investopedia. Investopedia US, n.d. Web. 08 Jan. 2014.

8. Anthony, Jillian. "Americans Receive Less Vacation Time in 2012." CNNMoney. Cable News Network, 16 Nov. 2012. Web. 08 Jan. 2014.

9. "Wells Fargo/Gallup: More than Half of Small Business Owners Work At Least Six-Day Weeks, Still Find Time for Personal Life." WellsFargo.com. Wells Fargo, 9 Aug. 2005. Web. 8 Jan. 2014.

10. Achor, Shawn. "Shawn Achor: The Happy Secret to Better Work." TED: Ideas worth Spreading. TED Conferences, LLC, Feb. 2012. Web. 05 Jan. 2014.

11. Maddalena, Laurie J., MBA, CPCC, PHR. "NextGen Know-How: Combating Negativity and Gossip." CU Management. CUES, 8 May 2013. Web. 08 Jan. 2014.

12. Schwartz, Tony. "Relax! You'll Be More Productive." NYTimes. com. New York Times, 9 Feb. 2013. Web. 8 Jan. 2014.

13. Fournier, Gillian. "Locus of Control | Encyclopedia of Psychology." Psych Central.com. Psych Central, 28 July 2010. Web. 08 Jan. 2014.

Chapter 4

1. Blumberg SJ, Luke JV. Wireless Substitution: Early release of estimates from the National Health Interview Survey, January–

June 2012. National Center for Health Statistics. December 2012. Available from: http://www.cdc.gov/nchs/nhis.htm.

2. Kanaracus, Chris. "Air Force Scraps Massive ERP Project after Racking up $1B in Costs." Computerworld.com. Computerworld Inc., 14 Nov. 2012. Web. 08 Jan. 2014.

3. Goldband, Bernie. "The Real Reasons Why ERP Systems Fail." The Real Reasons Why ERP Systems Fail. Noria Corporation, n.d. Web. 08 Jan. 2014.

4. Levick, Richard S. "3 Marketing Takeaways From Dollar Shave Club's F***ing Great Ad | Fast Company | Business Innovation." Fast Company. 2013 Mansueto Ventures, LLC., 23 Apr. 2012. Web. 08 Jan. 2014.

5. Miller, Mark. "Here Come the Boomer Biz Owners." WealthManagement.com Home Page. Penton, 11 Jan. 2013. Web. 08 Jan. 2014.

6. Rosenberg, Joyce M. "Retiring Boomers Driving Sales of Small Businesses." Yahoo Small Business Advisor. Yahoo!, 15 May 2013. Web. 09 Jan. 2014.

7. Miller, Mark. "Here Come the Boomer Biz Owners." WealthManagement.com Home Page. Penton, 11 Jan. 2013. Web. 08 Jan. 2014.

8. Barker, Eric. "Why You're Only Productive For Three Days Of The Work Week."Business Insider. Business Insider, Inc., 31 May 2012. Web. 09 Jan. 2014.

9. Goman, Carol Kinsey. "The Myth of Multitasking." Forbes. Forbes Magazine, 26 Apr. 2011. Web. 09 Jan. 2014.

10. Sollisch, Jim. "Multitasking Makes Us a Little Dumber." Chicago Tribune. The Tribune Company, 10 Aug. 2010. Web. 09 Jan. 2014.

11. Schiff, Lewis. "7 Habits of the Ultra Wealthy." Inc.com. Mansueto Ventures, 19 Mar. 2013. Web. 09 Jan. 2014.

12. Kaplan, Soren. "6 Ways To Create A Culture Of Innovation | Co.Design | Business Design." FastCompany.com. Mansueto Ventures, LLC, 12 Dec. 2013. Web. 09 Jan. 2014.

13. "People and Discoveries: Ford Installs the First Moving Assembly Line." PBS.org. PBS, n.d. Web. 07 Jan. 2014.

14. "Drive by Daniel Pink - Book Review." MarshallCF.com. Marshall Commercial Funding, n.d. Web. 9 Jan. 2014.

Chapter 5

1. Thomas, G. Scott. "Recession Claimed 170,000 Small Businesses in Two Years." BizJournals.com. American City Business Journals, 24 Jul. 2012. Web. 09 Jan. 2014.

2. Moyer, Melinda Wenner. "Successful Salespeople Have Moderate Temperaments: Scientific American." www.scientificamerican.com. Scientific American, Inc., 27 Jan. 2013. Web. 09 Jan. 2014.

3. Mallin, Michael L., Edward O'Donnell, and Michael Y. Hu. "How Do I Trust Thee: Let Me Control the Way." Journal of Selling & Major Account Management. Northern Illinois University, Fall 2007. Web. 9 Jan. 2014.

4. Kelley, Donna J., Slavica Singer, and Mike Herrington. "Global Entrepreneurship Monitor: 2011 Global Report." www. gemconsortium.org. Global Entrepreneurship Monitor, 2011. Web. 9 Jan. 2014.

5. Buxton, Cheryl. "Tips for Taking Assessment Tests." Http://online. wsj.com/. Wall Street Journal, 17 July 2009. Web. 9 Jan. 2014.

6. Handler, Charles, PhD, and Steven Hunt, PhD. "Assessment Tools." Workforce.com. MediaTec Publishing Inc., 28 Nov. 2002. Web. 09 Jan. 2014.

Chapter 6

1. Trout, Jack. "Peter Drucker On Marketing." Forbes. Forbes Magazine, 3 July 2006. Web. 09 Jan. 2014.

2. Nanji, Ayaz. "How Running a Small Business Has Changed [Infographic]."MarketingProfs.com. Marketing Profs, LLC, 19 June 2013. Web. 09 Jan. 2014.

3. Zeitlin, Matthew. "Why Groupon and LivingSocial Are

Doomed." The Daily Beast. Newsweek/Daily Beast, 30 Nov. 2012. Web. 09 Jan. 2014.

4. Donnelly, Tim. "How to Narrow Your Target Market BY Tim Donnelly." Inc.com. Mansueto Ventures, 20 Apr. 2011. Web. 09 Jan. 2014.

5. Beesley, Caron. "How to Set a Marketing Budget That Fits Your Business Goals." SBA.gov. Small Business Administration, 9 Jan. 2013. Web. 08 Jan. 2014.

6. Boykin, George. "What Percentage of Gross Revenue Should Be Used for Marketing & Advertising?" Smallbusiness.chron.com. Hearst Communications, Inc., 2009. Web. 09 Jan. 2014.

Chapter 7

1. Murninghan, J. Keith. "The Hands-off Approach to Leadership." The Globe and Mail. The Globe and Mail Inc., 14 Aug. 2012. Web. 09 Jan. 2014.

2. Kouzes, James M., and Barry Z. Posner. "To Lead, Create a Shared Vision." To Lead, Create a Shared Vision. Harvard Business Review, Jan. 2009. Web. 08 Jan. 2014.

3. Stewart, Hazel. "Want Successful Change Management? Get Employee Buy-In! | Wilson Learning India." Want Successful Change Management? Get Employee Buy-In! | Wilson Learning India. Wilson Learning India, 7 Sept. 2012. Web. 09 Jan. 2014.

4. "State of the American Workplace: Employee Engagement Insights for U.S. Business Leaders." State of the American Workplace. Gallup Inc., 2013. Web. 09 Jan. 2014.

5. Stell, R. "Preventing Employee Theft." NFIB.com. National Federation of Independent Business. 25 July 2006. Web. 09 Jan. 2014.

6. Kim, S.J., and S. Byrne. "Conceptualizing Personal Web Usage in Work Contexts: A Preliminary Framework." www.academia.edu. Computers in Human Behavior, 2011. Web. 09 Jan. 2014.

7. "2013 Mobility Survey by Allied." Allied.com. Allied Van Lines, Inc., 2013. Web. 09 Jan. 2014.

8. Hopper, Tom. "DNR - The Assembly Line and the $5 Day - Background Reading."www.michigan.gov/dnr. State of Michigan, 18 Aug. 2010. Web. 07 Jan. 2014.

9. Smith, Ned. "If You Listen Up, Your Employees Will Step Up." BusinessNewsDaily.com. TechMedia Network, 19 Jan. 2012. Web. 09 Jan. 2014.

10. Bacher, Jessica. "Employee Retention Still a Risky Issue for Companies Today." The Seamless Workforce. Yoh, 12 Oct. 2012. Web. 09 Jan. 2014.

11. "Smart Strategies to Avoid a Bad Hire." BBC.com. BBC, Inc., 19 July 2013. Web. 9 Jan. 2014.

12. Jager, Rama Dev, and Rafael Ortiz. "Steve Jobs: Hiring the Best Is Your Most Important Task." BusinessWeek.com. Bloomberg, L.P., 30 Oct. 1998. Web. 9 Jan. 2014.

13. Seward, Christopher. "Gallup: Blame Managers for Disengaged Workers." www.ajc.com. Atlanta Journal Constitution | Cox Media Group, 24 June 2013. Web. 9 Jan. 2014.

Chapter 8

1. Allen, James, Frederick F. Reichheld, Barney Hamilton, and Rob Markey. "Closing the Delivery Gap." www.bain.com. Bain & Company, 2005. Web. 9 Jan. 2014.

2. Loechner, Jack. "Poor Customer Service Costs Companies $83 Billion Annually." Mediapost.com/publications. The Center for Media Research, 18 Feb. 2010. Web. 9 Jan. 2014.

3. Allen, James, Frederick F. Reichheld, Barney Hamilton, and Rob Markey. "Closing the Delivery Gap." www.bain.com. Bain & Company, 2005. Web. 9 Jan. 2014.

4. "Tony Hsieh: Redefining Zappos' Business Model." www.BusinessWeek.com. Bloomberg, L.P., 27 May 2010. Web. 9 Jan. 2014.

5. Cerny, Jeff. "10 questions on customer service and "delivering happiness": an interview with Tony Hsieh." Tech Republic. October 1, 2009. Web. 9 Jan. 2014.

6. Exceptional Service, Exceptional Profit: The Secrets of Building a Five-Star Customer Service Organization, Leonardo Inghilleri and Micah Solomon, Amacom Books (New York), p. 116, 2010

7. "Customer Service and Business Results: A Survey of Customer Service from Mid-Size Companies." Zendesk.com. Dimensional Research, Apr. 2013. Web. 9 Jan. 2014.

8. Allen, James, Frederick F. Reichheld, Barney Hamilton, and Rob Markey. "Closing the Delivery Gap." www.bain.com. Bain & Company, 2005. Web. 9 Jan. 2014.

9. Allen, James, Frederick F. Reichheld, Barney Hamilton, and Rob Markey. "Closing the Delivery Gap." www.bain.com. Bain & Company, 2005. Web. 9 Jan. 2014.

10. Fuscaldo, Donna. "How to Get Customers to Come Back." Fox Small Business Center. FOX News Network, LLC, 26 Apr. 2013. Web. 09 Jan. 2014.

11. Kimbarovsky, Ross. "The Magic of Owning a Customer-Service Problem." Entrepreneur. Entrepreneur Media, Inc., 24 July 2013. Web. 09 Jan. 2014.

12. Huebsch, Russell. "Standard Employee Turnover in the Call Center Industry." Houston Chronicle Small Business. Hearst Communications, Inc., n.d. Web. 09 Jan. 2014.

13. Fairchild, Caroline. "Zappos' 10-Hour Long Customer Service Call Sets Record." The Huffington Post. TheHuffingtonPost.com, 21 Dec. 2012. Web. 09 Jan. 2014.

14. Jackson, Anna-Louise. "Domino's 'Brutally Honest' Ads Offset Slow Consumer Spending." BusinessWeek.com. Bloomberg, L.P., 17 Oct. 2011. Web. 9 Jan. 2014.

15. "Stories of Good and Bad Customer Service." SimpleComplexity. com. Simple Ideas, LLC., 13 Nov. 2010. Web. 9 Jan. 2014.

16. Gallo, Carmine. "Apple's Secret Employee Training Manual

Reinvents Customer Service in Seven Ways." Forbes. Forbes
Magazine, 30 Aug. 2012. Web. 09 Jan. 2014.

Chapter 9

1. "Data, Data Everywhere." TheEconomist.com. The Economist
Newspaper Limited, 25 Feb. 2010. Web. 9 Jan. 2014.

2. "Your Brain on Books: 10 Things That Happen to Our Minds
When We Read."OEDB.org. OEDb, 16 Jan. 2013. Web. 9 Jan. 2014.

3. Paul, Annie Murphy. "The Neuroscience of Your Brain on
Fiction." www.NYTimes.com. The New York Times Company, 17
Mar. 2012. Web. 9 Jan. 2014.

4. Bronson, Po. "How We Spend Our Leisure Time." TIME.com.
Time Inc., 23 Oct. 2006. Web. 9 Jan. 2014.

5. "American Time Use Survey Summary." www.BLS.gov. U.S. Bureau
of Labor Statistics, 20 June 2013. Web. 9 Jan. 2014.

6. Riggs, Ransom. "Who Reads Books?" Mental Floss. Mental Floss,
25 Apr. 2011. Web. 9 Jan. 2014.

7. "State of the Media Trends in TV Viewing - 2011." www.nielson.
com. The Nielson Company, 2011. Web. 9 Jan. 2014.

8. "New Research Reveals Many Entrepreneurs Are
Dyslexic." American Management Association. AMA—American
Management Association, 23 Jan. 2008. Web. 9 Jan. 2014.

9. Coppola, Gabriellle. "Why Dyslexics Make Great
Entrepreneurs." BusinessWeek.com. Bloomberg, L.P., 12 Dec. 2007.
Web. 09 Jan. 2014.

10. Elizabeth Walker, Janice Redmond, Beverley Webster, Megan Le
Clus, "Small business owners: too busy to train?" Journal of Small
Business and Enterprise Development. Vol. 14 Iss: 2, pp. 294 – 306.
2007.

11. Moeller, Philip. "Why Learning Leads to Happiness." US News &
World Report. US News & World Report, LP, 10 Apr. 2012. Web. 9
Jan. 2014.

12. Dubner, Stephen J. "Why Is "I Don't Know" So Hard to Say?" Freakonomics.com. Freakonomics, LLC, 4 Jan. 2012. Web. 9 Jan. 2014.

13. Waldroop, James, and Timothy Butler. "November 1996." Harvard Business Review. Harvard Business School Publishing, Nov. 1996. Web. 9 Jan. 2014.

14. McGovern, J., Lindemann, M., Vergara, M., Murphy, S., Barber, L., and Warrenfeltz, R. "Maximizing the impact of executive coaching: Behavioral change, organizational outcomes, and return on investment." The Manchester Review, 6, 1, 1-9., 2001, Web. 9 Jan. 2014.

15. "The Human Brain - Exercise." The Human Brain - Exercise. The Franklin Institute, 2004. Web. 08 Jan. 2014.

16. NeerGaard, Lauran. "Scientists: Brain Use Slows Deterioration." ABC News. ABC News Internet Ventures, 25 July 2013. Web. 9 Jan. 2014.

17. NeerGaard, Lauran. "Scientists: Brain Use Slows Deterioration." ABC News. ABC News Internet Ventures, 25 July 2013. Web. 9 Jan. 2014.